SIMPLE SONGS
THE **EASIEST** EASY GUITAR SONGBOOK EVER

ISBN 978-1-4950-0929-7

HAL•LEONARD®

7777 W. BLUEMOUND RD. P.O. BOX 13819 MILWAUKEE, WI 53213

Visit Hal Leonard Online at
www.halleonard.com

ALSO AVAILABLE:

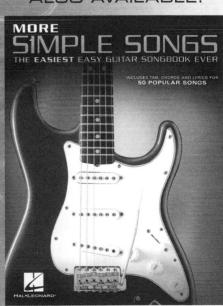

MORE SIMPLE SONGS
HL00172392

CONTENTS

Ain't No Sunshine

Words and Music by Bill Withers

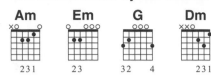

Key of Am
Verse
Slow

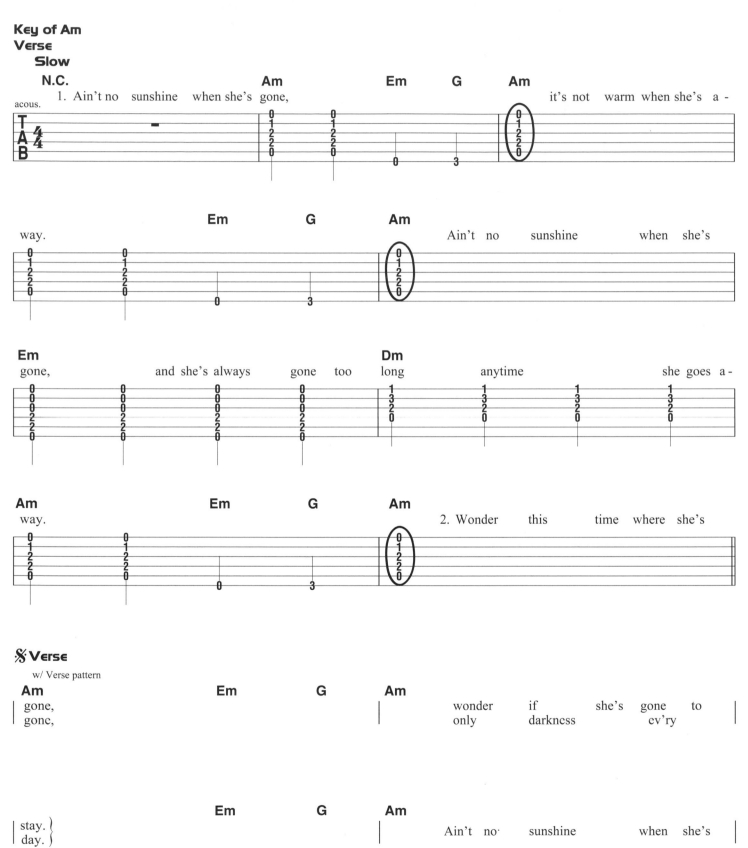

Em   **Dm**

| gone,   and   this   house   just   ain't   no | home   anytime   she   goes   a - |

To Coda ⊕

Am   **Em**   **G**   **Am**

| way. | And   I   know,   I   know,   I   know,   I   know, ‖

Bridge

N.C.

| I   know,   I   know,   I   know,   I   know,   I   know,   I | know,   I   know,   I   know,   I   know,   I   know,   I   know, |

| I   know,   I   know,   I   know,   I   know,   I   know, | I   know,   I   know,   I   know,   I   know,   I   know,   I |

| know,   hey,   I   ought   to   leave   the   young   thing   a - | lone,   but   ain't   no   sunshine   when   she's |

w/ Verse pattern   *D.S. al Coda*

Am   **Em**   **G**   **Am**

| gone. | 3. Ain't   no   sunshine   when   she's ‖

⊕ **Coda**   **Outro**

Am   **Am**   **Em**   **G**

| Anytime   she   goes   a - ‖: way. |

⌐ 1., 2. ————————————————————————— ⌐ 3. ————————————————————

Am   **Am**

| Anytime   she   goes   a - :‖ ◇   ‖

All Day and All of the Night

Words and Music by Ray Davies

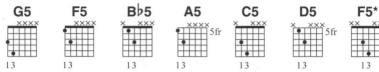

G5 F5 Bb5 A5 C5 D5 F5*

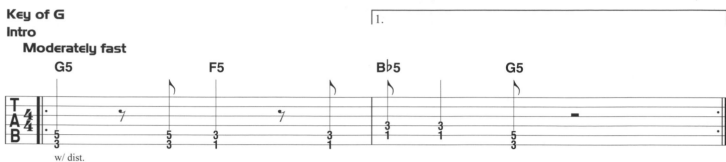

Key of G
Intro
Moderately fast

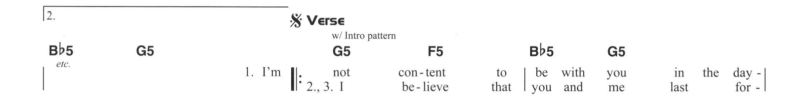

w/ dist.

% Verse
w/ Intro pattern

| G5 | F5 | Bb5 | G5 |

1. I'm not con‑tent to be with you in the day‑
2., 3. I be‑lieve that you and me last for‑

| F5 | Bb5 G5 | | F5 |

‑ time.
ever.   Oh, Girl, I want to

| Bb5 G5 | F5 Bb5 G5 |

be with you all of the time.}
night I'm yours, leave me never.}   The

Pre-Chorus

| Bb5 | F5 | A5 G5 |

on‑ly time I feel alright is by your side.

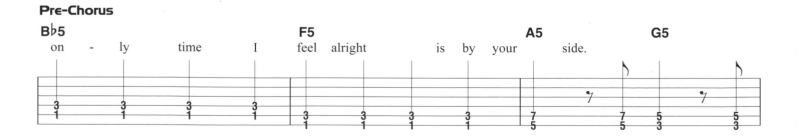

Chorus

C5   A5   D5   C5   F5*   D5

Girl,   I   want   to   be with   you   all of the

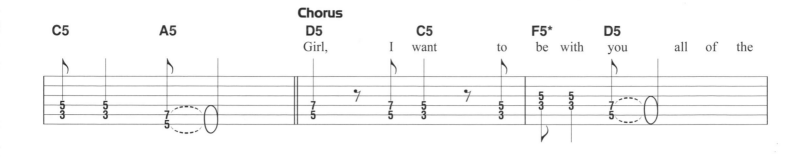

etc.   C5   F5*   D5   C5

time. All day   and | all of the night.   All day   and

3rd time, To Coda ⊕ |1.

F5*   D5   C5   F5*   D5

all of the night.   All day   and | all of the night.

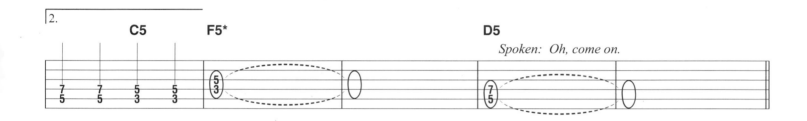

|2.   C5   F5*   D5

Spoken: Oh, come on.

Guitar Solo
w/ Intro pattern |1. - 4. ||5.   *D.S. al Coda*

||: G5   F5 |Bb5   G5   :|| Bb5   G5

⊕ **Coda**

D5   C5   F5*   D5

All day   and | all of the night.

C5   F5*   D5

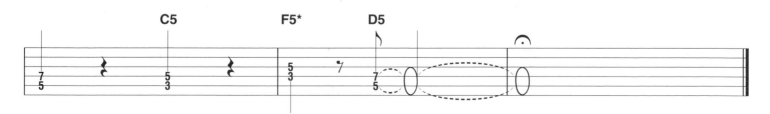

Beat It

Words and Music by Michael Jackson

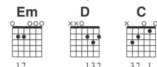

Em   D   C

Tune down 1/2 step:
(low to high) Eb-Ab-Db-Gb-Bb-Eb

Key of Em
Intro
Moderately fast

w/ dist.

%Verse

	Em	D	Em
1.	They told him, "Don't you ever	come a-round here. Don't	wanna see your face; you better
2.	They're out to get you. Better	leave while you can. Don't	wanna be a boy; you wanna
3.	*Guitar solo*		

	D	C	D
	dis-ap-pear." The	fire's in their eyes and their	words are really clear. So
	be a man. You	wanna stay a-live; better	do what you can. So

	Em	D	Em
	beat it, just	beat it.	You better run; you better
	beat it, just	beat it.	You have to show them that you're

	D	Em	D
	do what you can. Don't	wanna see no blood. Don't be a	macho man. You
	really not scared. You're	playin' with your life. This ain't no	"truth or dare." They'll

	C	D	Em
	wanna be tough; better	do what you can. So	beat it. But you
	kick you, then they'll beat you, then they'll	tell you it's fair. So	beat it. But you

D

wanna   be   bad.
wanna   be   bad.
Guitar Solo ends

Em

Just | beat it.   (Beat it.)

D

| Beat it.   (Beat it.)   No |

Em

one wants to be defeat |- ed.

D

Show | - in' how funky,   strong |

Em

3rd time, To Coda ✛

D

| is your fight.   It | does-n't   matter   who's | wrong or   right.   Just |

Em

1.

D

| beat it.   (Beat it.) Just |

Em

beat it. (Beat it.)   Just |

D

beat it.   (Beat it.) Just |

beat it. (Beat it, uh!)   :||

Em

2.

D

| beat it.   (Beat it.) |

Em

Beat it.   (Beat it.)   No |

D

one wants to be defeat |- ed.   Show -|

Em

D

| - in' how funky, strong | is your fight.   It |

Em

does-n't   matter   who's |

D

wrong or   right. Just ||

Bridge

w/ Voc. ad lib. on repeats

4th time, D.S. al Coda

Em

beat it.   Beat it.

Play 4 times

✛ **Coda**

Em

||: beat it.   (Beat it.) |

D

Beat it.   (Beat it.)   No |

Em

one wants to be defeat |- ed.   Show -|

D

Em

| - in' how funky, strong | is your fight.   It |

Em

does-n't   matter   who's |

D

Repeat and fade

wrong or   right. Just   :||

Blitzkrieg Bop

Words and Music by Jeffrey Hyman, John Cummings, Douglas Colvin and Thomas Erdelyi

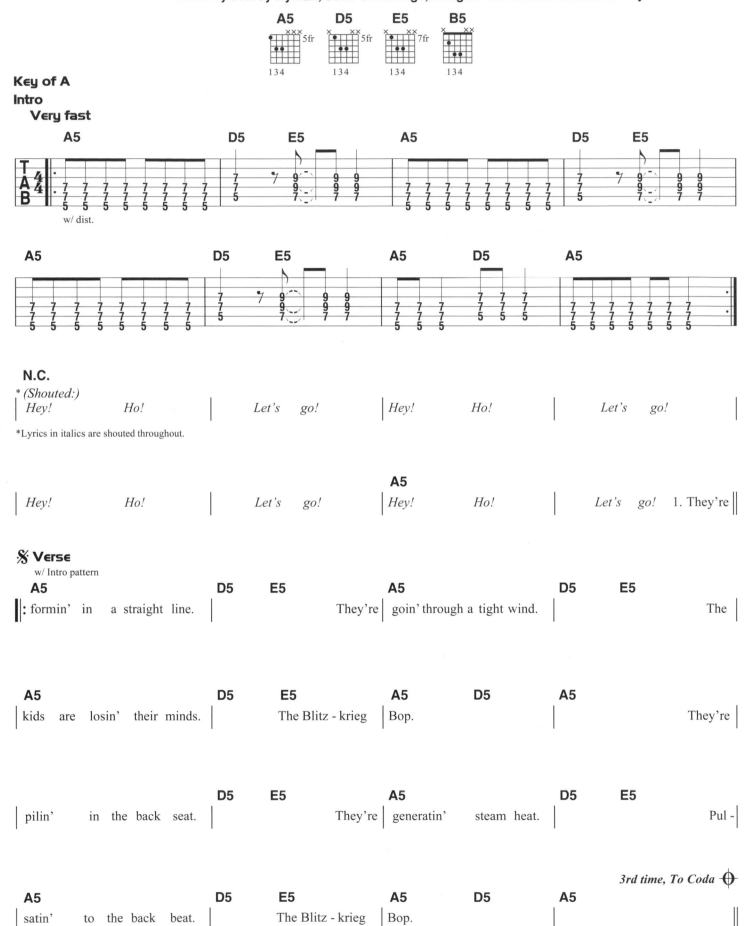

Key of A
Intro
Very fast

N.C.

* (Shouted:)
| Hey! Ho! | Let's go! | Hey! Ho! | Let's go! |

*Lyrics in italics are shouted throughout.

| Hey! Ho! | Let's go! | Hey! Ho! | Let's go! 1. They're |

Verse
w/ Intro pattern

A5 | D5 E5 | A5 | D5 E5 |
formin' in a straight line. | They're goin' through a tight wind. | The |

A5 | D5 E5 | A5 D5 | A5 |
kids are losin' their minds. | The Blitz - krieg Bop. | They're |

| D5 E5 | A5 | D5 E5 |
pilin' in the back seat. | They're generatin' steam heat. | Pul - |

3rd time, To Coda

A5 | D5 E5 | A5 D5 | A5 |
satin' to the back beat. | The Blitz - krieg Bop. |

Bridge

D5					A5	D5	A5	
Hey!	Ho!			Let's go!	Shoot 'em in the back, now.			

2nd time, D.S. al Coda

D5					B5	D5	E5	
What	they	want,	I don't	know. They're	all revved up and	ready	to go. 2., 3. They're	:

⊕ Coda

Outro

N.C.

Hey!	Ho!		Let's go!	Hey!	Ho!		Let's go!	

A5

Hey!	Ho!		Let's go!	Hey!	Ho!		Let's go!	

Chasing Cars

Words and Music by Gary Lightbody, Tom Simpson, Paul Wilson, Jonathan Quinn and Nathan Connolly

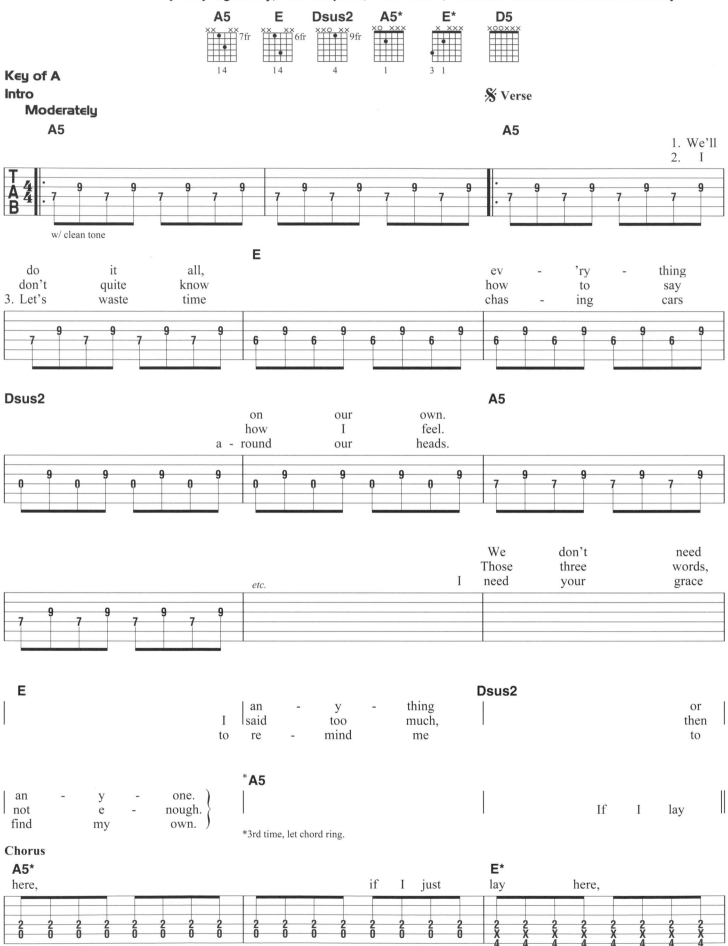

12

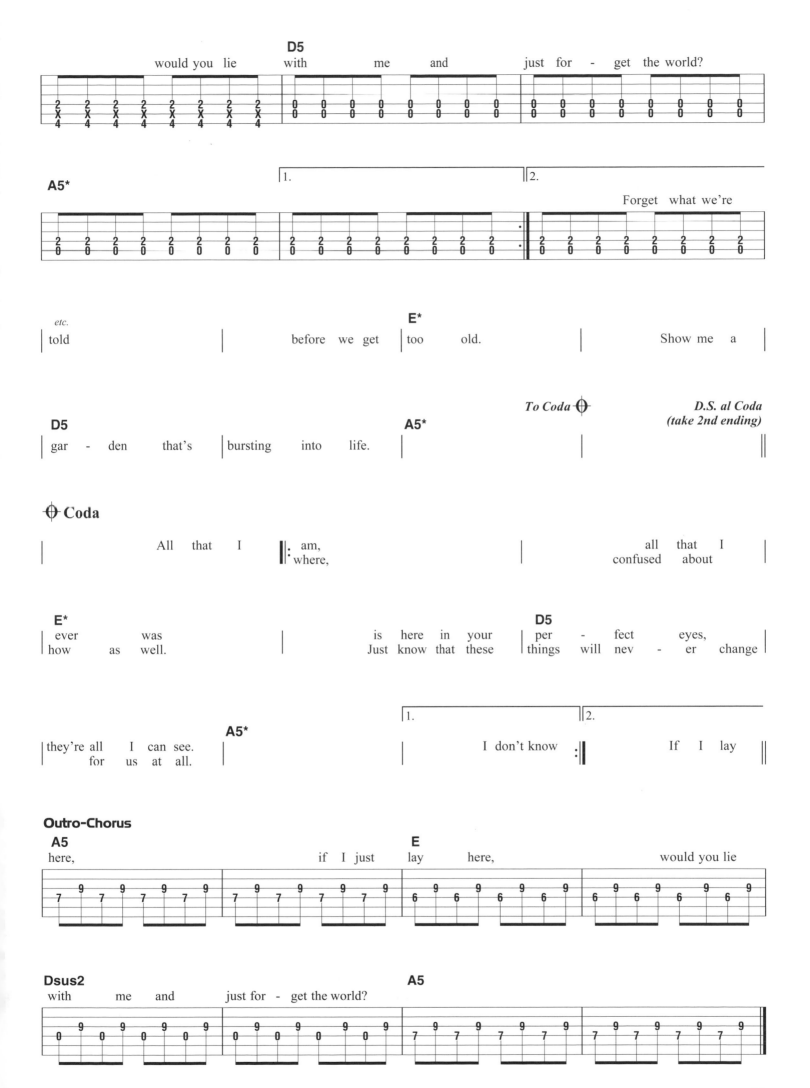

Every Rose Has Its Thorn

Words and Music by Bobby Dall, C.C. Deville, Bret Michaels and Rikki Rockett

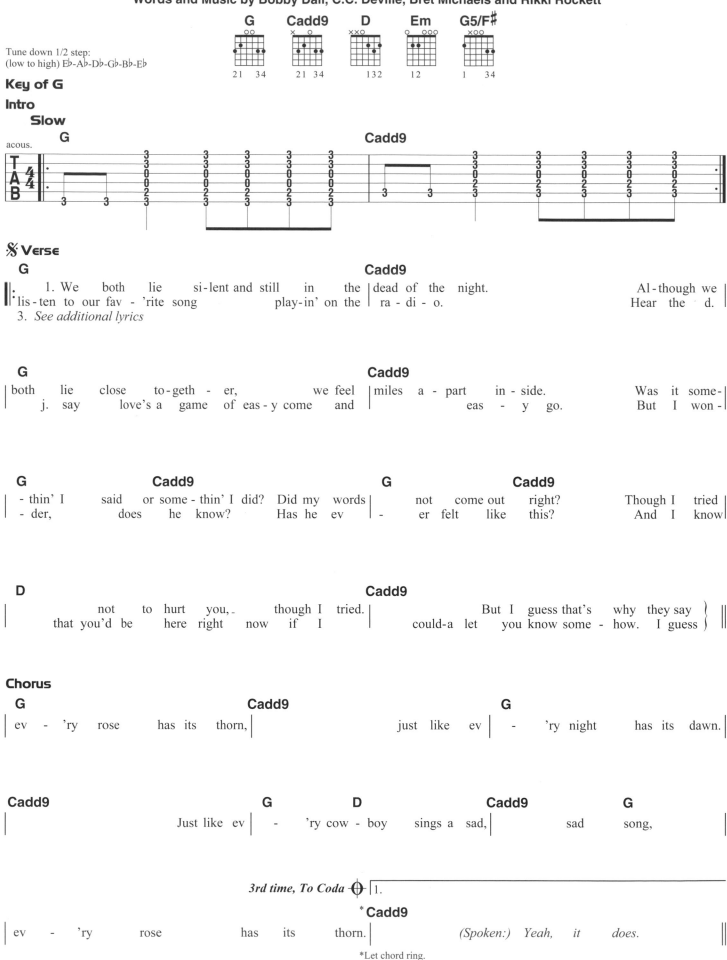

14

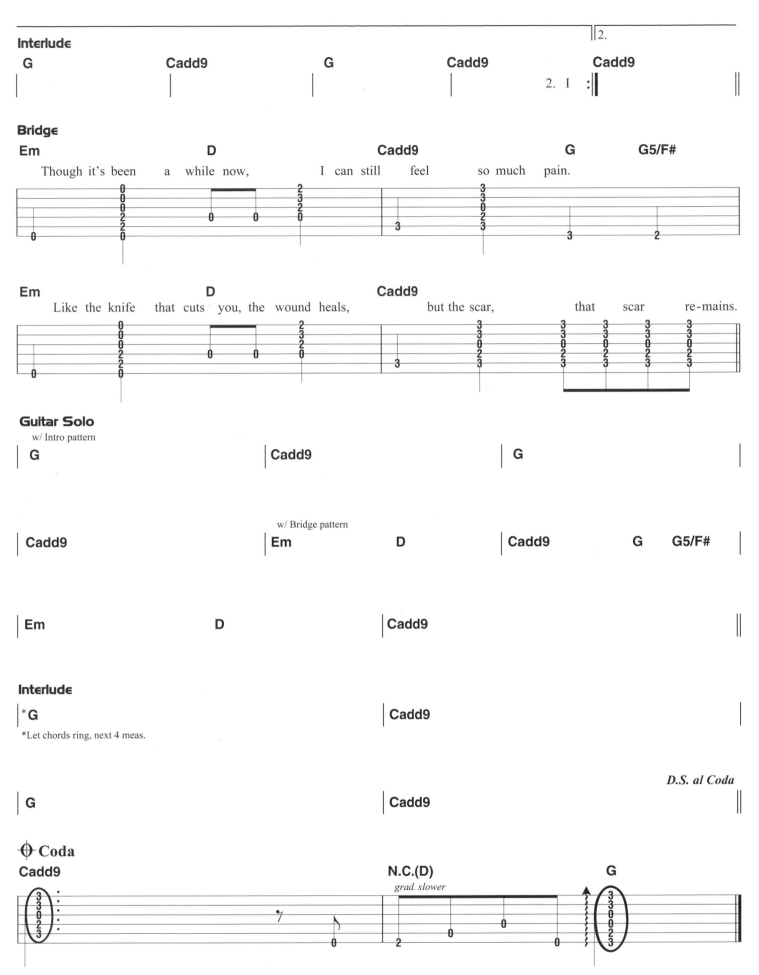

Additional Lyrics

3. I know I coulda saved a love that night if I'd known what to say.
   'Stead of makin' love, we both made our sep'rate ways.
   And now I hear you found somebody new and that I never meant that much to you.
   To hear that tears me up inside and to see you cuts me like a knife.
   I guess...

Everybody Hurts

Words and Music by William Berry, Peter Buck, Michael Mills and Michael Stipe

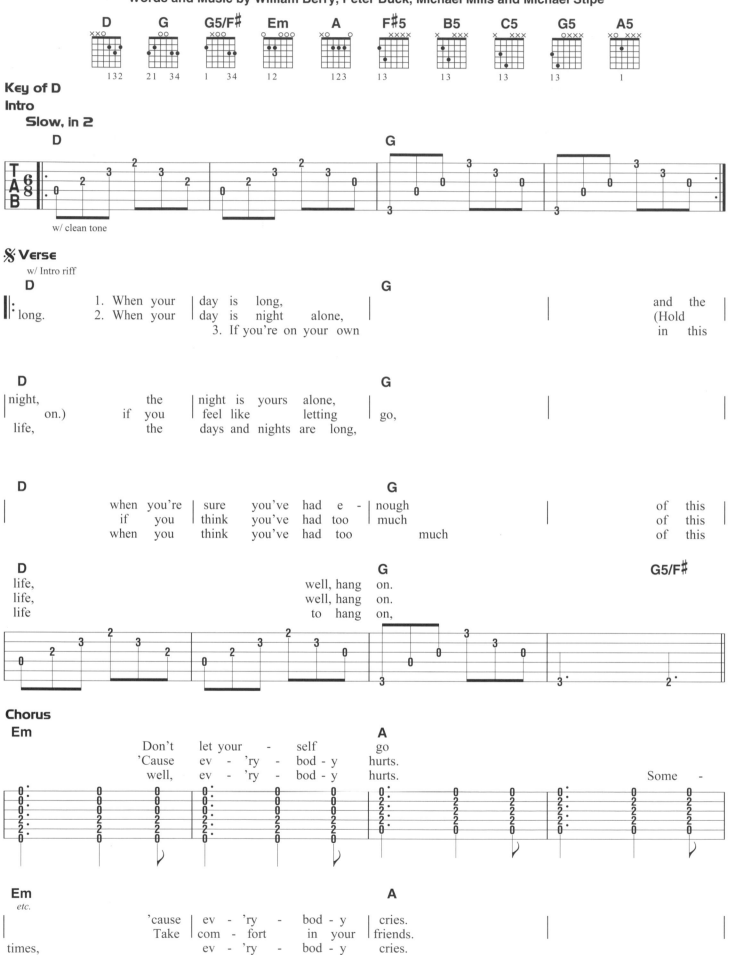

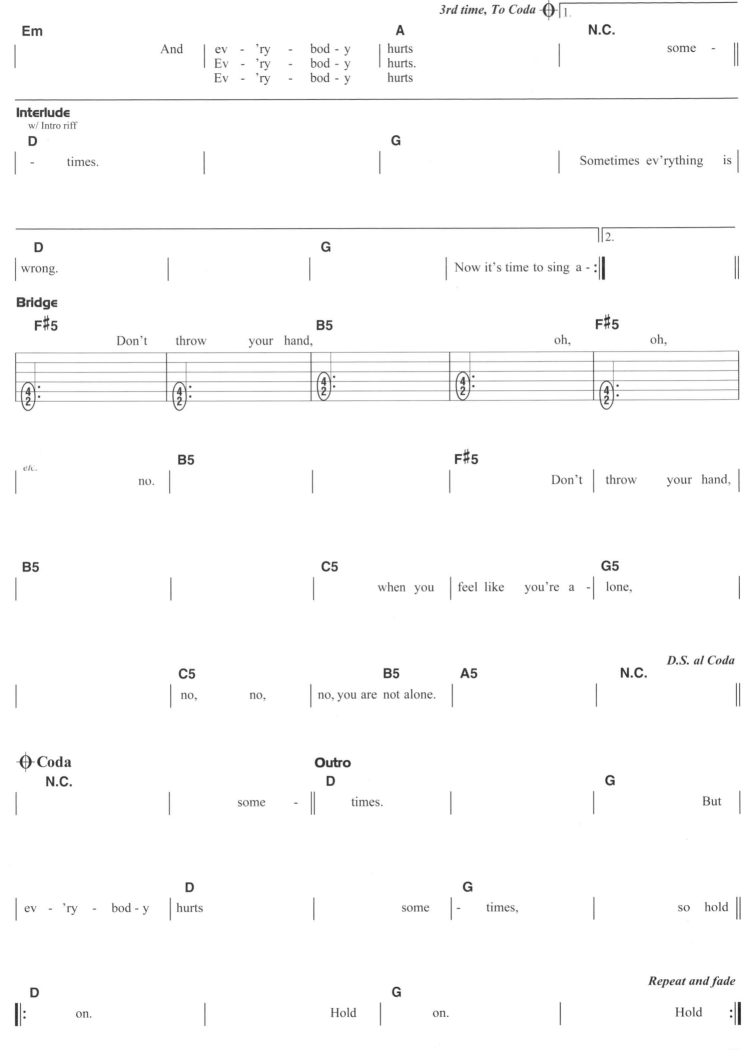

Folsom Prison Blues

Words and Music by John R. Cash

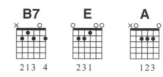

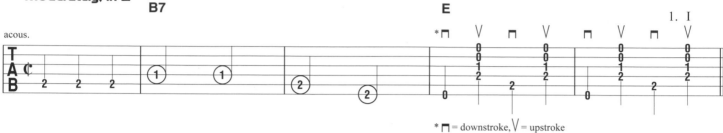

Capo I

Key of F (Capo Key of E)
Intro
    Moderately, in 2

* ⊓ = downstroke, V = upstroke

Verse
    E
    etc.

‖: hear the train a com | - in',   it's | rollin' 'round the bend, | and |
2nd & 3rd times, Guitar Solo

| I ain't seen the sun | - shine   since | I don't know | when.   I'm |

A
| stuck in Folsom | prison | and time keeps | draggin' on. |

E
| | | | But that |

B7
| train keeps a roll | - in', | on down to | San An - |

Verse

E

tone.				2. When I ‖	**E**			
				3. I ‖ bet there's	rich folks	eatin'	from a	fan-
			4. Well, if they	freed	me from this	prison,	if	that

(2.) When I ‖ was just a ba | - by, my

mama	told	me,	"Son,		always	be a	good	boy,	don't
-cy	dining	car;		they're	prob'bly	drinkin' cof	-fee	and
railroad	train	was	mine,		I	bet I'd	move	it all	a	little

A

ever	play with	guns."	But I	shot	a man	in	Reno
smoking	big cigars.		Well, I	know	I	had it	comin',
farther	down the	line.		Far	from	Folsom	prison,

E

just	to	watch	him	die.
I know I		can't	be	free.
that's where I		want	to	stay.

B7

When I	hear that	whistle	blowing,
But those	people	keep a mov	- in',
And I'd	let that	lonesome	whistle

E | 1., 2. |

I	hang my	head	and	cry.	:‖
and	that's what	tortures		me.
blow	my	blues	a	- way.

| 3.

B7　　　　　　　　　**E**

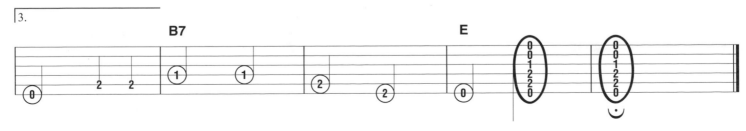

Free Fallin'

Words and Music by Tom Petty and Jeff Lynne

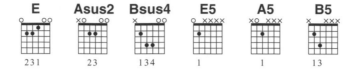

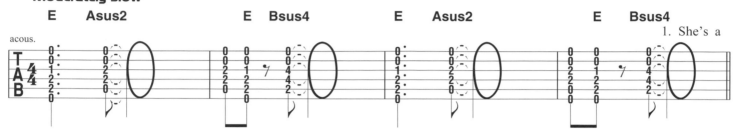

Capo I

Key of F (Capo Key of E)
Intro
  Moderately slow

Verse

E	Asus2		E	Bsus4		E	Asus2
good	girl,		loves	her mama,	loves	Je -	sus	and A -

E	Bsus4		E	Asus2		E	Bsus4	
merica	too.	She's a	good	girl,		crazy 'bout	Elvis,	loves

E	Asus2		E	Bsus4	E	Asus2	E	Bsus4
hors - es	and her	boyfriend too.					2. And it's a

𝄋 Verse

E	Asus2		E	Bsus4		There's a
long	day		livin' in Reseda.			
vam -	pires		walkin' through the valley		move
glide	down		over Mulholland,		I wanna

E	Asus2		E	Bsus4	
free -	way		runnin' through the yard.	And I'm a
west	down	Ven -	tura Boulevard.	And all the
write	her		name in the sky.	I'm gonna

E	Asus2		E	Bsus4	
bad	boy	'cause I	don't even miss her.	I'm a
bad	boys	are	standin' in the shadows.	And the
free	fall	out into	nothin',	gonna

3rd time, To Coda ⊕

E	Asus2		E	Bsus4	
bad	boy	for	breakin' her heart.	And }
good	girls	are	home with broken hearts.	Now } I'm
leave	this	world for a	while.	Now

Chorus

| E Asus2 | E Bsus4 | E Asus2 | E Bsus4 |

free, | | free | fallin'. | | Yeah, I'm

| E Asus2 | E Bsus4 | E Asus2 | 1. / E Bsus4 | 2. / E Bsus4 |

free, | | free | fallin'. | 3. Now all the | |

Interlude

| E Asus2 | E Bsus4 | E Asus2 | E Bsus4 |

| | (Free fallin', I'm a | free fallin', I'm a... |

D.S. al Coda

| E Asus2 | E Bsus4 | E Asus2 | E Bsus4 |

| | Free fallin', I'm a | free fallin', I'm...) 4. I wanna |

⊕ Coda

Chorus

| E Asus2 | E Bsus4 | E Asus2 | E Bsus4 |

free, | (Fallin', I'm a | free fallin', I'm a free | fallin'. | free fallin', I'm a | Yeah, I'm free fallin', I'm a... |

| E Asus2 | E Bsus4 | E Asus2 | E Bsus4 |

free, | Fallin', I'm a | free fallin', I'm a free | fallin'. | free fallin', I'm a | free fallin', I'm a...) |

Interlude

| E5 A5 | E5 B5 | E5 A5 | E5 B5 |

| | (Free fallin', I'm a | free fallin', I'm a...) | Yeah, I'm

```
|----------------------------|--------------------|------------------------|--------------------------|
|----------------------------|--------------------|------------------------|--------------------------|
|--------2---2-------2---2----|----2---2---4-4-4-4--|--------2---2---2---2----|----2---2---4-4-4-4-|
|-2-2-2------2-0-0-0---0-0----|-0-2-2---2-2-2-2-2-2-|-2-2-2------2-0-0-0-0----|-0-2-2---2-2-4-4-4--|
|-0-0-0---------0-0-0---------|------0-------------|-0-0-0---------0-0-0-----|------0-------------|
|----------------------------|--------------------|------------------------|--------------------------|
```

Outro-Chorus
w/ Intro pattern

Repeat and fade

| E Asus2 | E Bsus4 | E Asus2 | E Bsus4 |

‖: free, | | free | fallin'. | | Oh! :‖

* (Free fallin', I'm a | free fallin', I'm a | free fallin', I'm a | free fallin', I'm a...)

*Bkgds enter 2nd time.

Good Riddance (Time of Your Life)

Words by Billie Joe
Music by Green Day

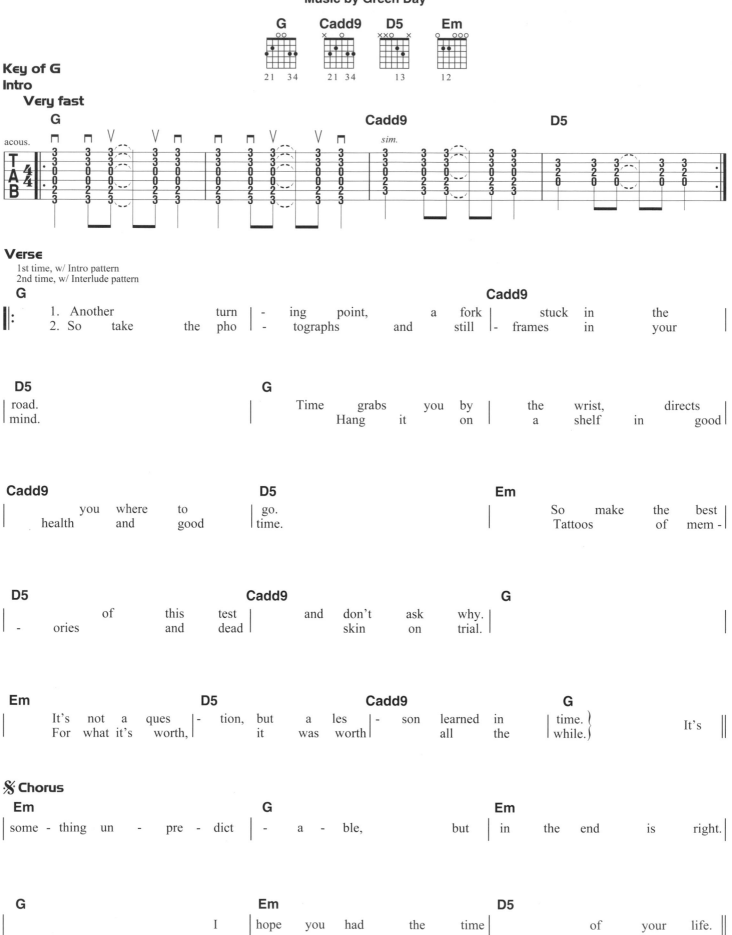

Key of G
Intro
Very fast

Verse

1st time, w/ Intro pattern
2nd time, w/ Interlude pattern

1. Another turning point, a fork stuck in the
2. So take the photographs and still frames in the your

road. Time grabs you by the wrist, directs
mind. Hang it on a shelf in good

you where to go. So make the best
health and good time. Tattoos of mem -

- ories of this test and don't ask why.
- ories and dead skin on trial.

It's not a question, but a lesson learned in time.
For what it's worth, it was worth all the while.

It's

Chorus

something unpredictable, but in the end is right.

I hope you had the time of your life.

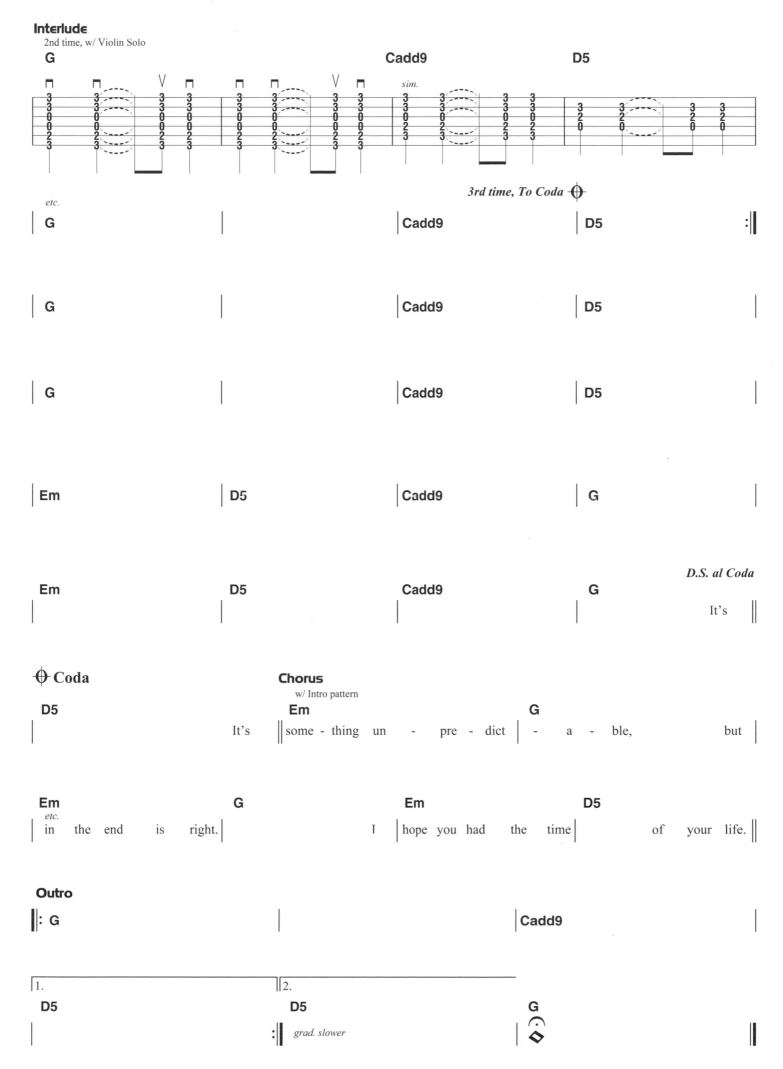

Interlude
2nd time, w/ Violin Solo

G   **Cadd9**   **D5**

sim.

etc.

3rd time, To Coda ⊕

| **G** | | **Cadd9** | **D5** | :‖

| **G** | | **Cadd9** | **D5** |

| **G** | | **Cadd9** | **D5** |

| **Em** | **D5** | **Cadd9** | **G** |

D.S. al Coda

| **Em** | **D5** | **Cadd9** | **G** |
| | | | It's ‖

⊕ **Coda**

D5

| | It's ‖

Chorus
w/ Intro pattern

Em   **G**

‖ some - thing un - pre - dict | - a - ble, but |

Em   **G**   **Em**   **D5**

etc.

| in the end is right. | | I | hope you had the time | of your life. ‖

Outro

‖: **G** | | **Cadd9** |

|1.
D5

|2.
D5   **G**

:‖ *grad. slower* ⬥ ‖

23

Hallelujah

Words and Music by Leonard Cohen

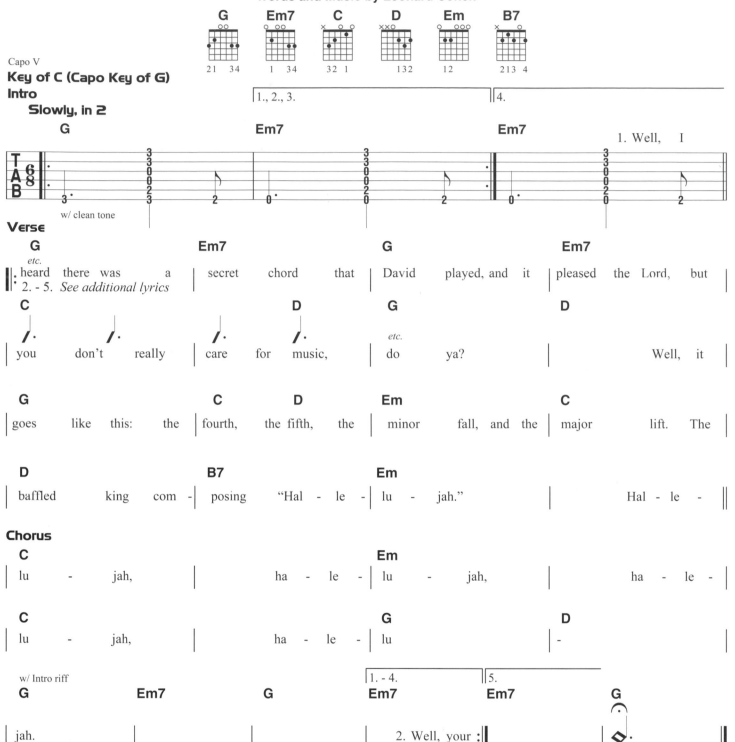

Capo V

Key of C (Capo Key of G)

Intro

Slowly, in 2

w/ clean tone

Verse

|: heard there was   a | secret   chord   that | David   played, and it | pleased   the Lord, but |
2. - 5. *See additional lyrics*

| you   don't   really | care   for   music, | *etc.* do   ya? | Well,   it |

| goes   like   this: the | fourth,   the fifth,   the | minor   fall, and the | major   lift.   The |

| baffled   king   com - | posing   "Hal - le - | lu - jah." | Hal - le - :||

Chorus

| lu - jah, | ha - le - lu - jah, | ha - le - |

| lu - jah, | ha - le - lu | - |

w/ Intro riff

| jah. | | | 2. Well, your :|| | |

Additional Lyrics

2. Well, your faith was strong but you needed proof.
You saw her bathing on the roof.
Her beauty and the moonlight overthrew ya.
And she tied you to her kitchen chair,
And she broke your throne and cut your hair,
And from your lips she drew the hallelujah.

3. Well, baby, I've been here before,
I've seen this room and I've walked this floor,
You know, I used to live alone before I knew ya.
And I've seen your flag on the marble arch,
And love is not a vict'ry march,
It's a cold and it's a broken hallelujah.

4. Well, there was a time when you let me know
What's really going on below.
But now you never show that to me, do ya?
But remember when I moved in you
And the holy dove was moving too,
And ev'ry breath we drew was hallelujah.

5. Maybe there is a God above,
But all I've ever learned from love
Was how to shoot somebody who outdrew ya.
And it's not a cry that you hear at night,
It's not somebody who's seen the light,
It's a cold and it's a broken hallelujah.

The House of the Rising Sun

Words and Music by Alan Price

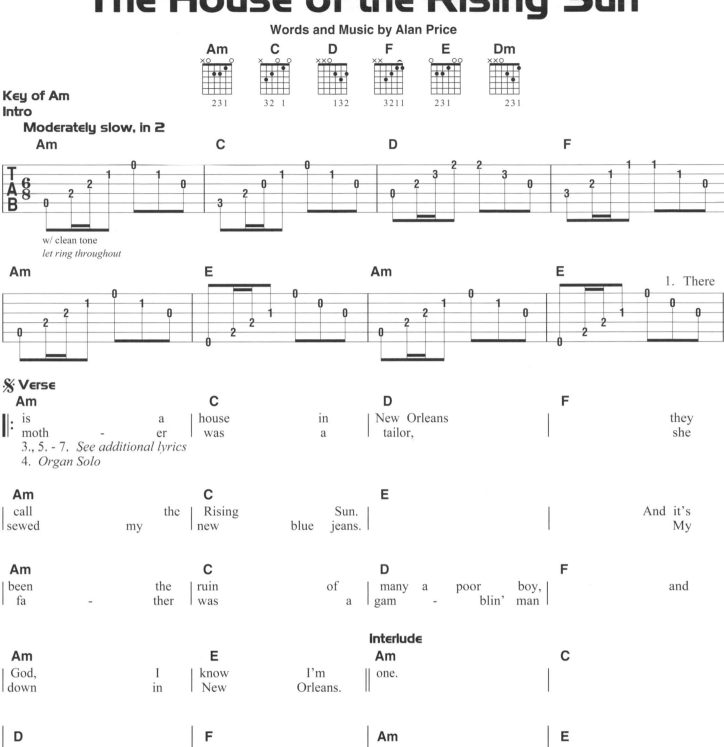

Key of Am
Intro

Moderately slow, in 2

w/ clean tone
let ring throughout

1. There

Verse

Am	C	D	F	
is a	house in	New Orleans		they
moth - er	was a	tailor,		she

3., 5. - 7. See additional lyrics
4. Organ Solo

Am	C	E		
call the	Rising Sun.			And it's
sewed my	new blue jeans.			My

Am	C	D	F	
been the	ruin of	many a poor boy,		and
fa - ther	was a	gam - blin' man		

Interlude

Am	E	Am	C
God, I	know I'm	one.	
down in	New Orleans.		

D	F	Am	E

Fine |1. - 5.| |6.| *D.S. al Fine*

Am	E	E	
		2. My	7. Well, there

Additional Lyrics

3. Now the only thing a gambler needs
is a suitcase and and trunk.
And the only time he's satisfied
Is when he's on a drunk.

5. Oh, mother, tell your children
Not to do what I have done,
Spend your lives in sin and misery
In the House of the Rising Sun.

6. Well, I got one foot on the platform,
The other foot on the train.
I'm goin' back to New Orleans
To wear that ball and chain.

7. Well, there is a house in New Orleans
They call the Rising Sun.
And it's been the ruin of many a poor boy,
And God, I know I'm one.

Have You Ever Seen the Rain?

Words and Music by John Fogerty

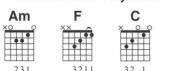

Am   F   C   G

Key of C

Intro

Moderately

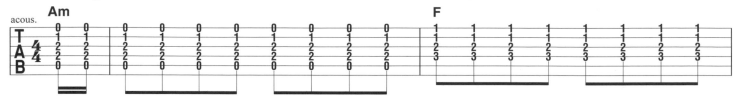

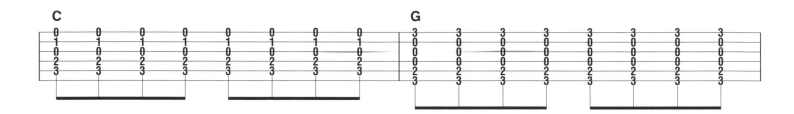

Verse

C

etc.

1. Someone told me long ago   there's a calm before
2. Yesterday and days ago before   sun is cold and rain

   the storm. I know,   it's been com - in' for
   is hard. I know,   been that way for all

   some time.   When it's o - ver, so
   my time.   Till for - ev - er, on

   they say,   it'll rain a sun - ny day. I know;
   it goes,   through the circle fast   and slow. I know;

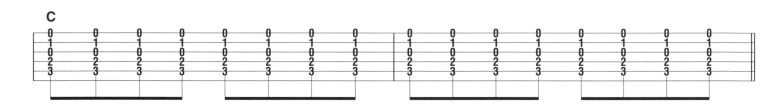

G   **C**

| shinin' down like | water.
| it can't stop, I won | - der.

Chorus

F   **G**   **C**   **Am**

I want to | know,   have you | ever   seen   the | rain?

F   **G**   **C**   **Am**

I want to | know,   have you | ever   seen   the | rain

F   **G**   **C**

comin' down | a sun-ny day? | | 1. | 2.

F   **G**   **C**   **Am**

I want to | know,   have you | ever   seen   the | rain?

F   **G**   **C**   **Am**

I want to | know,   have you | ever   seen   the | rain

F   **G**   **C**   **G**   **C**

comin' down | a sun-ny day? |

He's a Pirate

from Walt Disney Pictures' PIRATES OF THE CARIBBEAN: THE CURSE OF THE BLACK PEARL

Music by Klaus Badelt

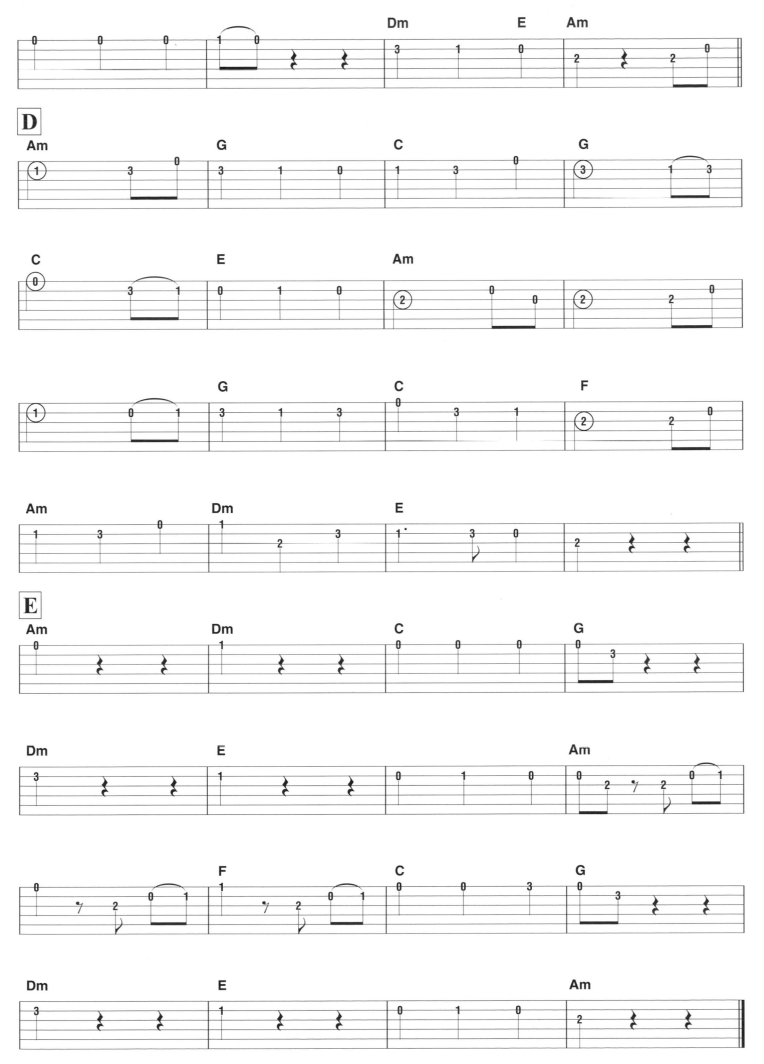

Helter Skelter

Words and Music by John Lennon and Paul McCartney

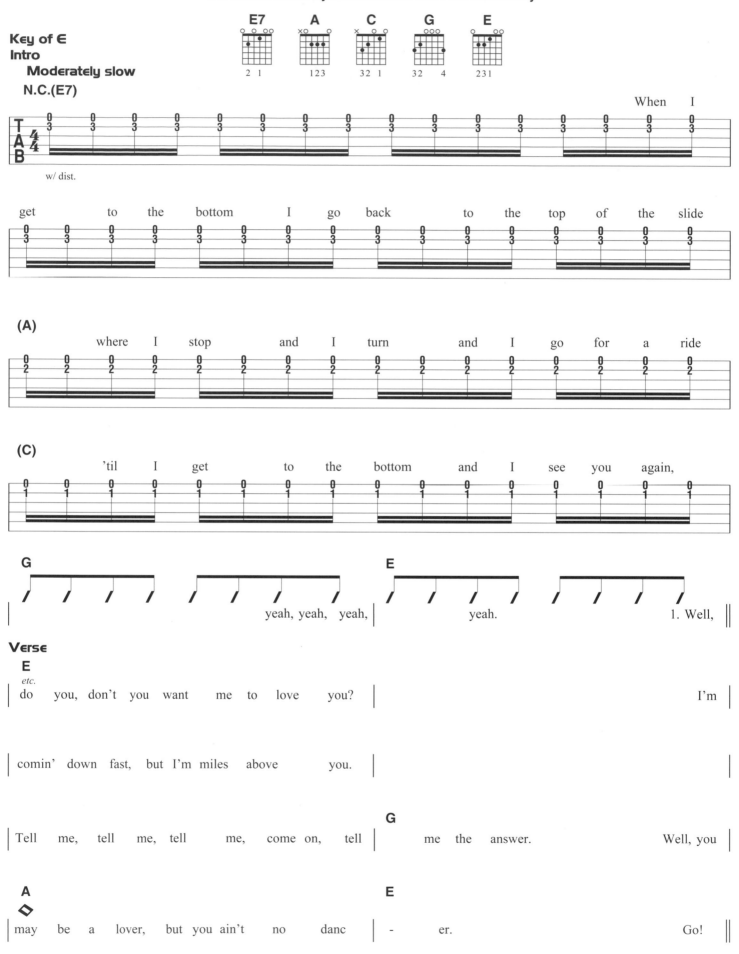

Key of E
Intro
  Moderately slow

30

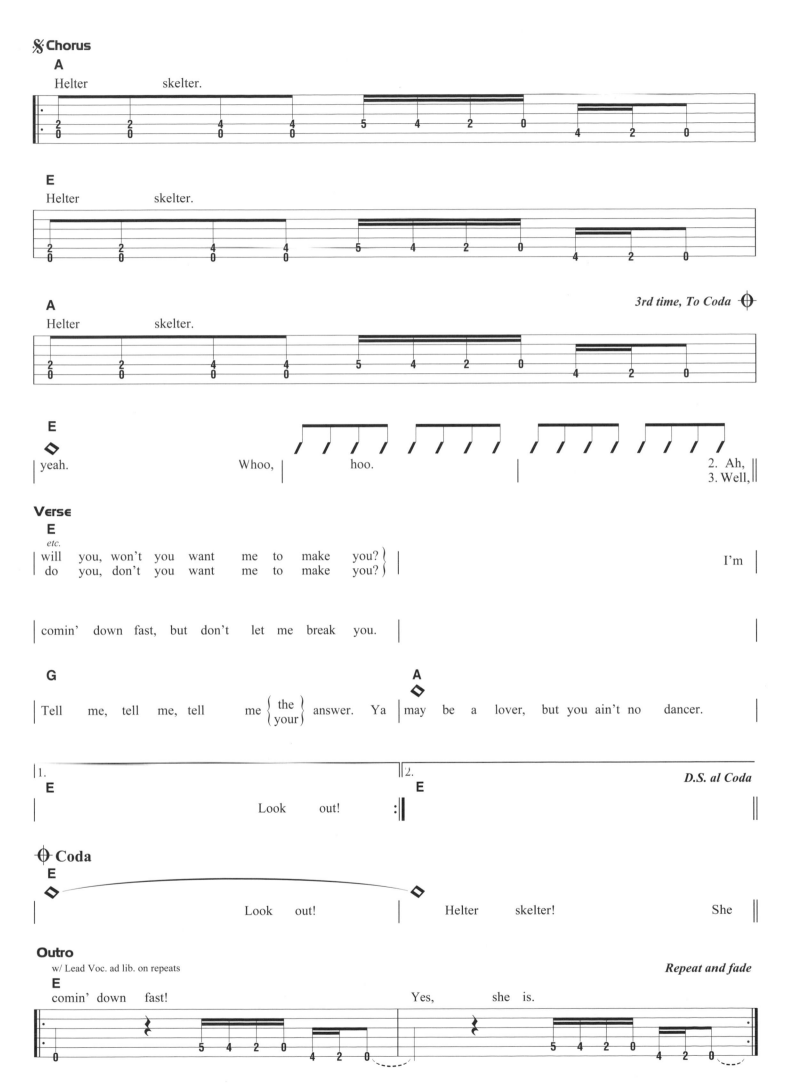

Highway to Hell

Words and Music by Angus Young, Malcolm Young and Bon Scott

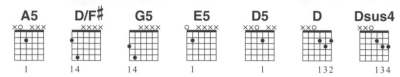

Key of A
Intro
Moderately

w/ dist.

Verse
w/ Intro pattern

A5	D/F# G5	D/F# G5
1. Livin' easy,	living free.	
2. No stop signs,	living speed limit.	

D/F# G5 D/F# A5		D/F# G5
Season ticket on a one-way ride.		Askin' nothing
No-body's gonna slow me down.		Like a wheel,

D/F# G5 D/F# G5 D/F# A5		
leave me be. Takin' ev'rything in my stride.		
gonna spin it. No-body's gonna mess me around.		

D/F# G5	D/F# G5 D/F# G5 D/F# A5	
Don't need reason, don't need rhyme.	Ain't nothin' I'd	
Hey, Satan, pay'n' my dues,	playin' in a	

D/F# G5	D/F# G5
rather do. Going down, party time,	
rockin' band. Hey, mama, look at me,	

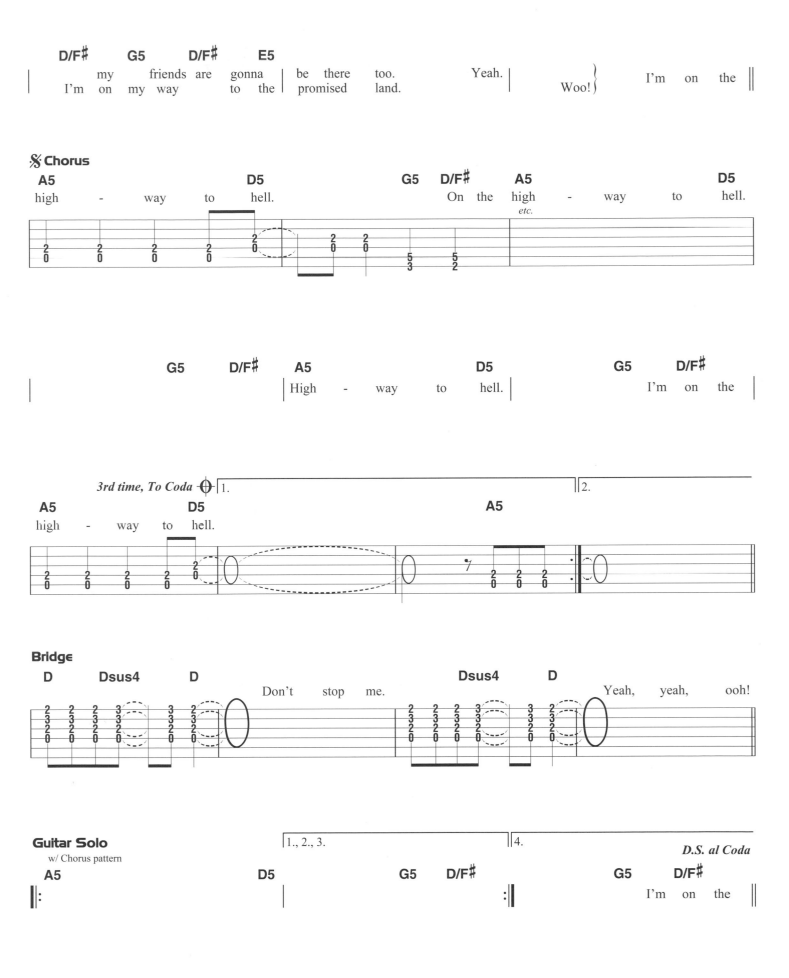

A Horse with No Name

Words and Music by Dewey Bunnell

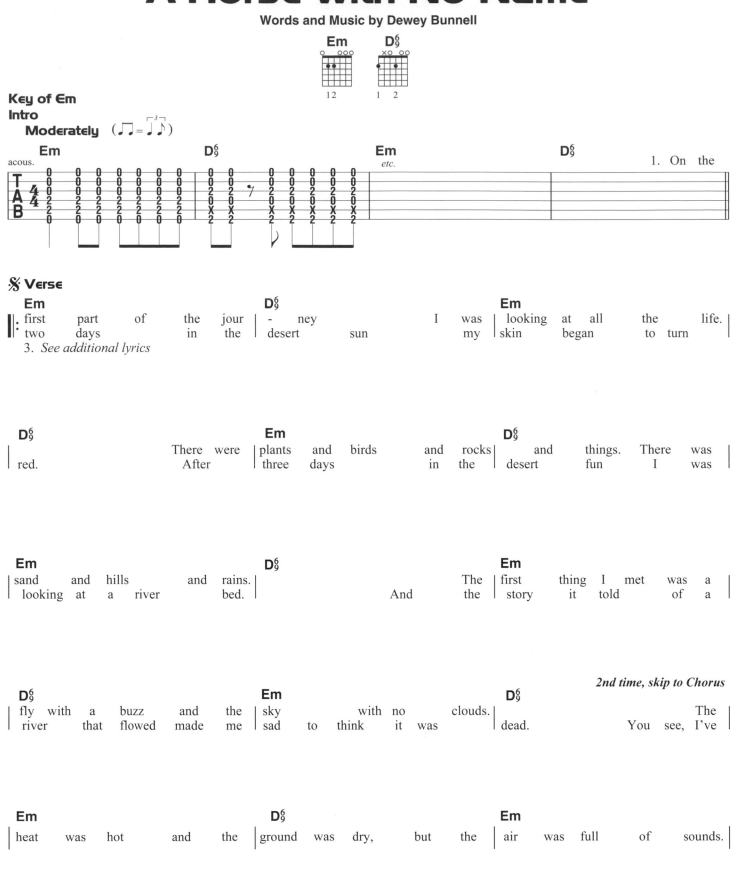

Key of Em
Intro
Moderately

first part of the jour-ney I was looking at all the life.
two days in the desert sun my skin began to turn

3. *See additional lyrics*

red. There were plants and birds and rocks and things. There was
After three days in the desert fun I was

sand and hills and rains. The first thing I met was a
looking at a river bed. And the story it told of a

2nd time, skip to Chorus

fly with a buzz and the sky with no clouds. The
river that flowed made me sad to think it was dead. You see, I've

heat was hot and the ground was dry, but the air was full of sounds.

Chorus

I've been through the desert on a horse with no name. It felt

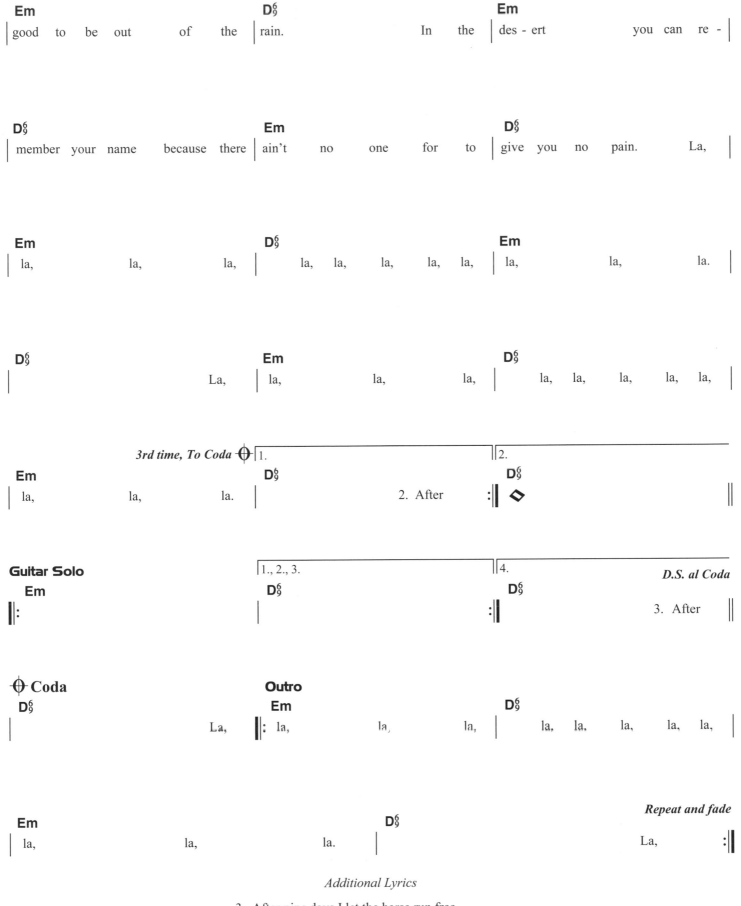

Em good to be out of the | **D⁶₉** rain. In the | **Em** des - ert you can re -

D⁶₉ member your name because there | **Em** ain't no one for to | **D⁶₉** give you no pain. La,

Em la, la, la, | **D⁶₉** la, la, la, la, la, | **Em** la, la, la.

D⁶₉ La, | **Em** la, la, la, | **D⁶₉** la, la, la, la, la,

3rd time, To Coda ⊕ |1.
Em la, la, la. | **D⁶₉** 2. After :|| ◇ |2. **D⁶₉** ||

Guitar Solo |1., 2., 3.
Em ||: | **D⁶₉** |4. **D⁶₉** :| *D.S. al Coda* 3. After ||

⊕ **Coda** **Outro**
D⁶₉ La, | **Em** ||: la, la, la, | **D⁶₉** la, la, la, la, la,

Repeat and fade
Em la, la, la. | **D⁶₉** La, :||

Additional Lyrics

3. After nine days I let the horse run free
   'Cause the desert had turned to sea.
   There were plants and birds and rocks and things.
   There was sand and hills and rains.
   The ocean is a desert with its life underground
   And the perfect disguise above.
   Under the cities lies a heart made of ground,
   But the humans will give no love.
   You see I've…

I Gotta Feeling

Words and Music by Will Adams, Allan Pineda, Jaime Gomez, Stacy Ferguson, David Guetta and Frederic Riesterer

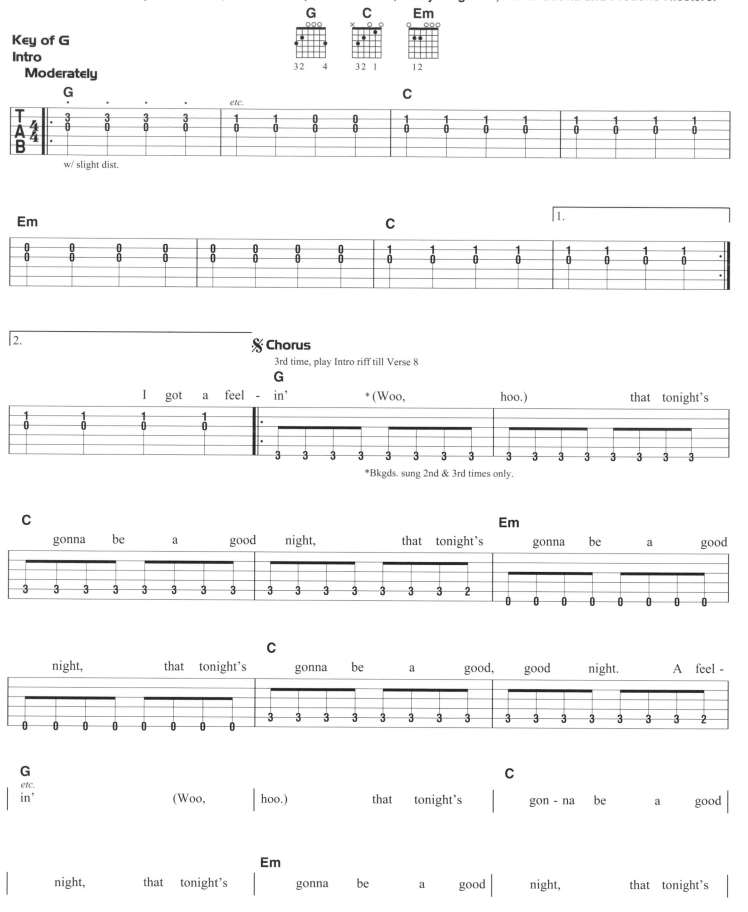

C

| gonna be a good, | good night. A feel - :‖ | good night. I feel... ‖

Verse

G   **C**

*Spoken:

| 1., 5. *Tonight's the night.* | *Let's live it up.* | *I got my money.* | *Let's spend it up.* |

*Lyrics in italics are spoken throughout.

Em   **C**

| *Go out and smash it.* | *Like, oh my God.* | *Jump off that sofa.* |

1st time only

Verse

N.C.   **C**   **G**

| *Let's get, get*   *off.* ‖ 2. I know that we'll | have a ball if we get |

C   **Em**

| down and go out and just | lose it all. I feel | stressed out. I wan - |

                    C   **N.C.**

| na let it go. Let's go way | out, spaced out and los - | ing all control. (Ch, ch, ch, ch.) ‖

Verse

G   **C**   **N.C.**

| 3., 6. *Fill up my cup.* | *Mazel tov!* | *Look at her dancing;* | *just take it off.* |

Em   **N.C.**   **C**

| *Let's paint the town.* | *We'll shut it down.* | *Let's burn the roof* |

Verse

                                     G

| and then we'll do it again. ‖ 4., 7. Let's do it, let's | do it, let's do it, let's do |

C   **Em**

| it, and do it, and | do it, let's live it up and | do it, and do it, and |

C

| do it, do it, do it. Let's | do it. Let's do it. Let's | do it, 'cause I gotta feel - ‖

⊕ **Coda**

Verse
w/ Chorus riff
G

| do it, do it, do it, do it. ‖ 8. *Here we come, here we go,* | *we gotta rock.* |

C   **Em**

| *Easy come, easy go.* | *Now we on top.* | *Feel the shot, body rock.* |

                        C

| *Rock it, don't stop.* | *'Round and 'round, up and down,* | *around the clock.* ‖

Verse
G   **C**

| 9. Monday, Tuesday, | Wednesday and Thursday. | Friday, Saturday, |

                        Em

| Saturday to Sunday. | Get, get, get, get, get with us. | You know what we say, say. |

Outro-Chorus
C   **G**

| Party ev'ry day. P - p - p - | party ev'ry day. And I'm feel- ‖: in' (Woo, |

                        C

| hoo.) that tonight's | gonna be a good | night, that tonight's |

Em   **C**

| gonna be a good | night, that tonight's | gonna be a good, |

| 1.   ‖ 2.
                                       *G
| good night. A feel -:‖ good night. | (Woo, | hoo.) ‖

*Let chord ring.

Knockin' on Heaven's Door

Words and Music by Bob Dylan

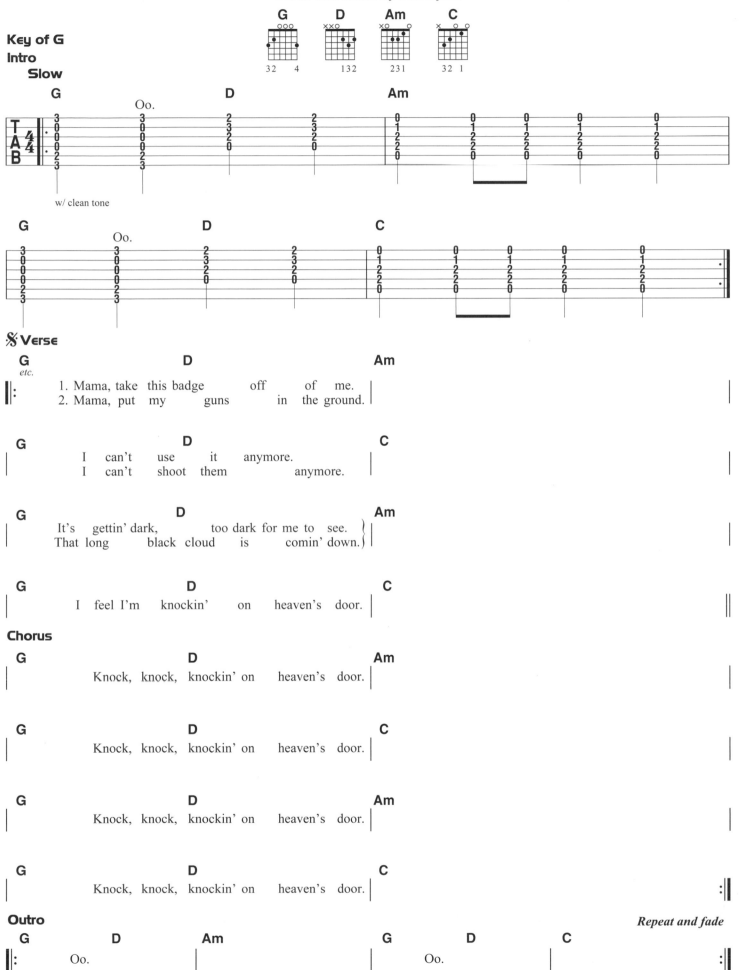

I Love Rock 'n Roll

Words and Music by Alan Merrill and Jake Hooker

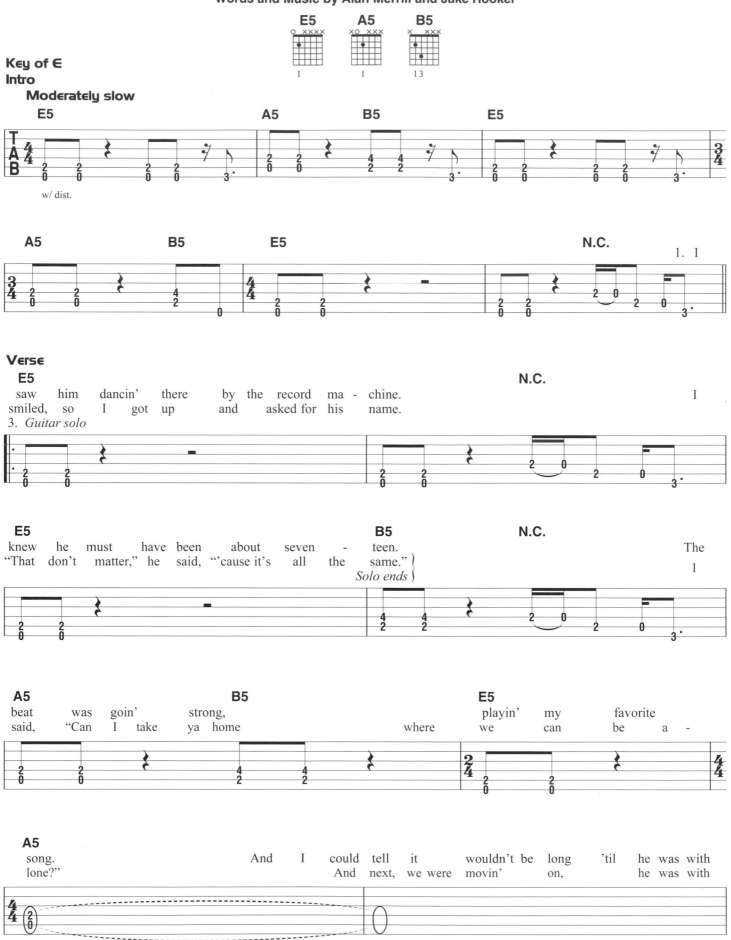

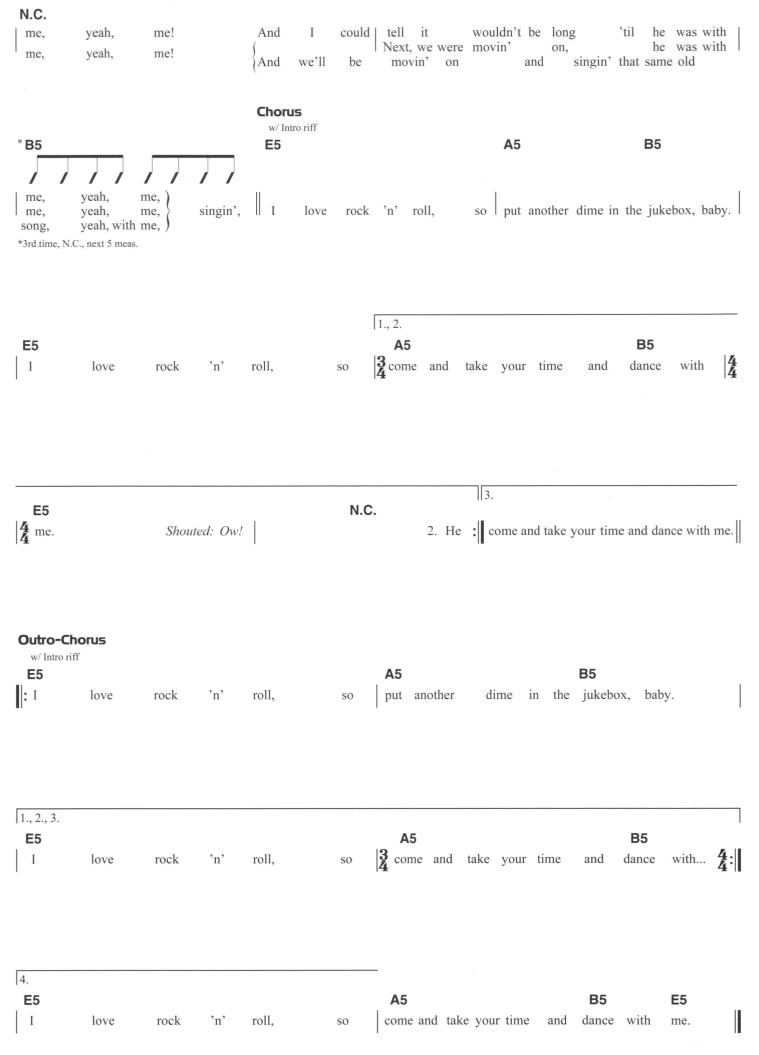

I'm Your Hoochie Coochie Man

Written by Willie Dixon

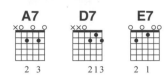

Key of A

Intro

Slow, in 4

A7

w/ clean tone

𝄌 Verse

A7

1. The gypsy woman told my mother before I was born,
2., 3. *See additional lyrics*

"You got a boy childs comin' gonna be a son - of - a - gun.

He gonna make pretty womens jump an' shout.

Then the world wanna know what this all about?" But you know I'm here,

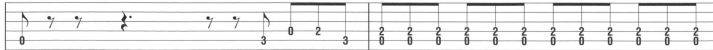

Chorus

3rd time, To Coda ⊕

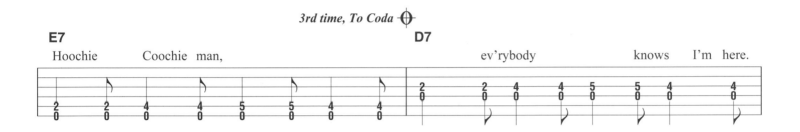

2nd time, D.S. al Coda

⊕ **Coda**

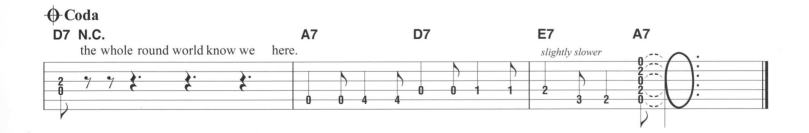

Additional Lyrics

2. I got a black cat bone, I got a mojo too.
I got the John the Conquerroot, I'm gonna mess with you.
I'm gonna make you girls lead me by my hand.
Then the world'll know that I'm the Hoochie Coochie man.

3. On the seventh hour, on the seventh day,
On the seventh month, the seventh doctor said,
"You were born for good luck, and that you'll see."
I got seven hundred dollars, and don't you mess with me.

I'm Yours

Words and Music by Jason Mraz

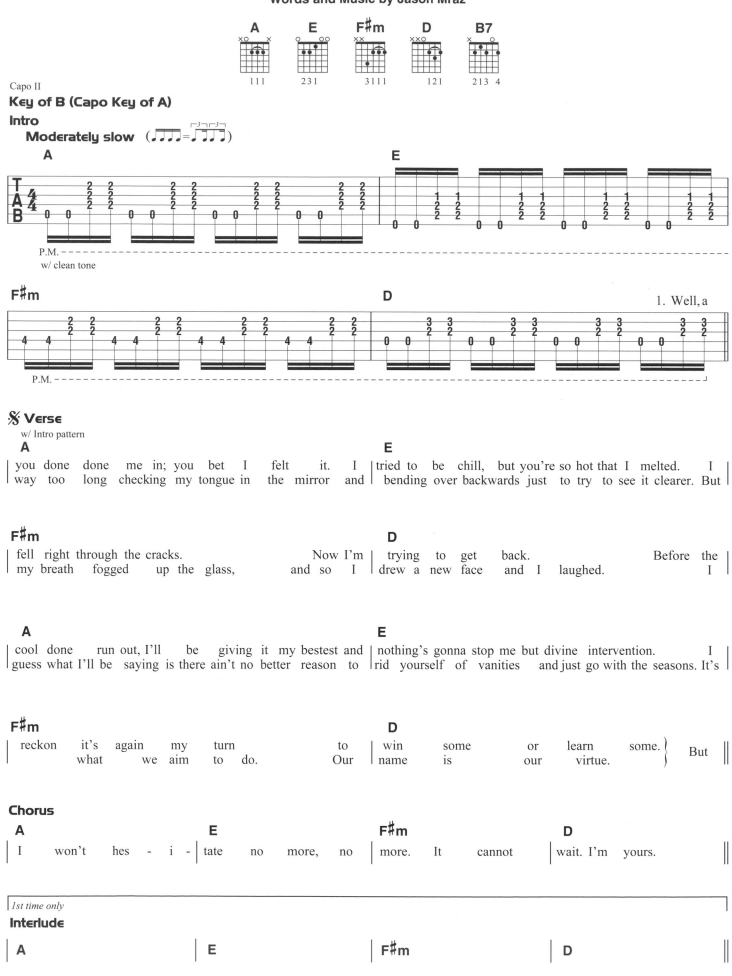

Capo II

Key of B (Capo Key of A)

Intro

Moderately slow

§ Verse

w/ Intro pattern

A

you done done me in; you bet I felt it. I | tried to be chill, but you're so hot that I melted. I

way too long checking my tongue in the mirror and | bending over backwards just to try to see it clearer. But

F♯m

fell right through the cracks. Now I'm | trying to get back. Before the

my breath fogged up the glass, and so I | drew a new face and I laughed. I

A

cool done run out, I'll be giving it my bestest and | nothing's gonna stop me but divine intervention. I

guess what I'll be saying is there ain't no better reason to | rid yourself of vanities and just go with the seasons. It's

F♯m

reckon it's again my turn to | win some or learn some. }

what we aim to do. Our | name is our virtue. } But

Chorus

A **E** **F♯m** **D**

I won't hes - i - | tate no more, no | more. It cannot | wait. I'm yours.

1st time only

Interlude

A | **E** | **F♯m** | **D** ‖

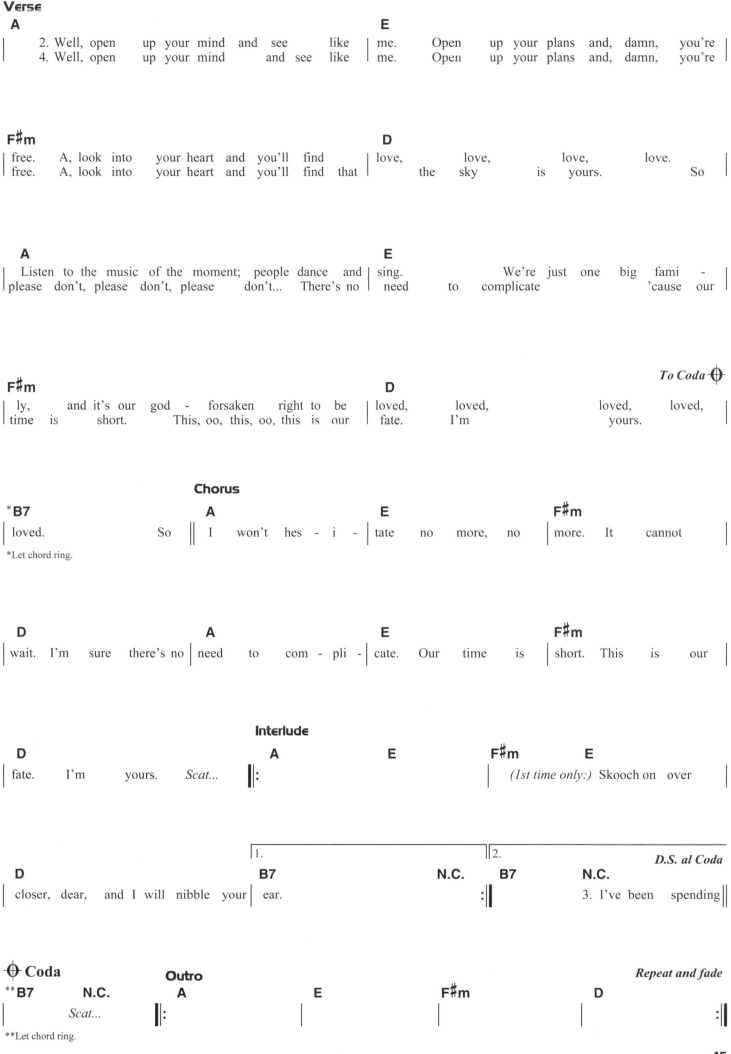

Verse

A   E

| 2. Well, open up your mind and see like | me. Open up your plans and, damn, you're |

| 4. Well, open up your mind and see like | me. Open up your plans and, damn, you're |

F♯m   D

| free. A, look into your heart and you'll find | love, love, love, love. |

| free. A, look into your heart and you'll find that | the sky is yours. So |

A   E

| Listen to the music of the moment; people dance and | sing. We're just one big fami - |

| please don't, please don't, please don't... There's no | need to complicate 'cause our |

To Coda ⊕

F♯m   D

| ly, and it's our god - forsaken right to be | loved, loved, loved, loved, |

| time is short. This, oo, this, oo, this is our | fate. I'm yours. |

Chorus

*B7   A   E   F♯m

| loved. So ‖ I won't hes - i - | tate no more, no | more. It cannot |

*Let chord ring.

D   A   E   F♯m

| wait. I'm sure there's no | need to com - pli - | cate. Our time is | short. This is our |

Interlude

D   A   E   F♯m   E

| fate. I'm yours. *Scat...* ‖: | *(1st time only:)* Skooch on over |

                                   1.   2.   *D.S. al Coda*

D   B7   N.C.   B7   N.C.

| closer, dear, and I will nibble your | ear. :‖ | 3. I've been spending ‖

⊕ **Coda**   **Outro**   *Repeat and fade*

**B7   N.C.   A   E   F♯m   D

| *Scat...* ‖: | | | | :‖

**Let chord ring.

In My Life

Words and Music by John Lennon and Paul McCartney

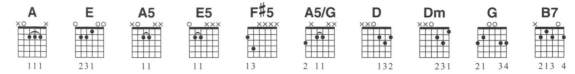

Key of A
Intro
Moderately

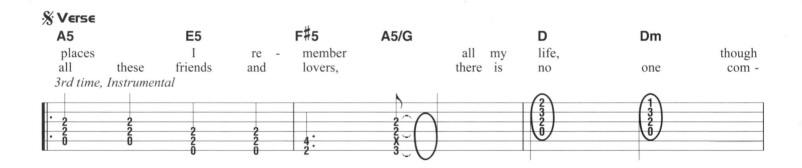

w/ clean tone

% Verse

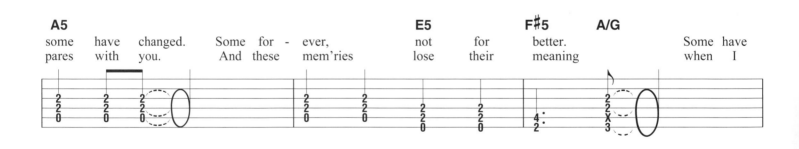

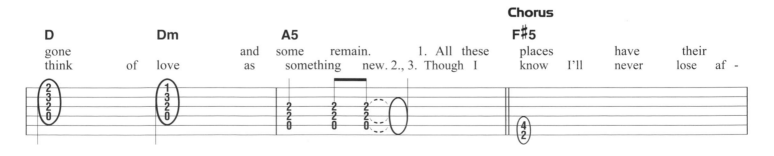

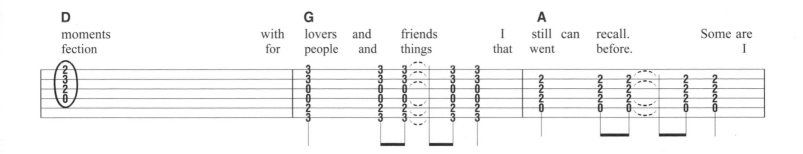

D   G   A

moments   with lovers and friends I still can recall.   Some are

fection   for people and things that went before.   I

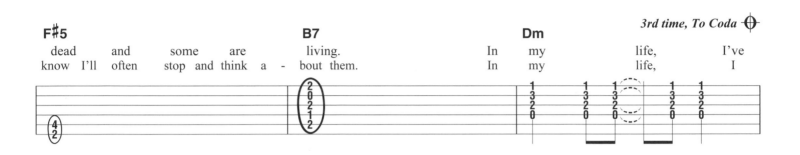

F#5   B7   Dm   *3rd time, To Coda*

dead and some are   living. In my   life,   I've

know I'll often stop and think a - bout them. In my   life,   I

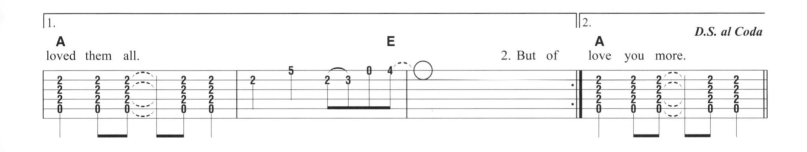

|1. |2.   *D.S. al Coda*

A   E   A

loved them all.   2. But of love you more.

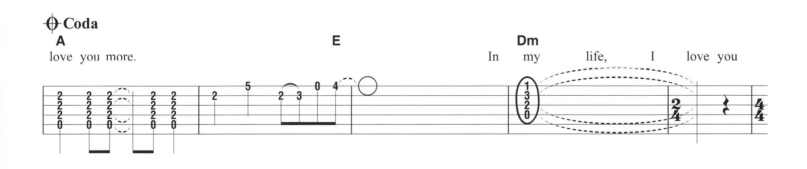

⊕**Coda**

A   E   Dm

love you more.   In my   life, I love you

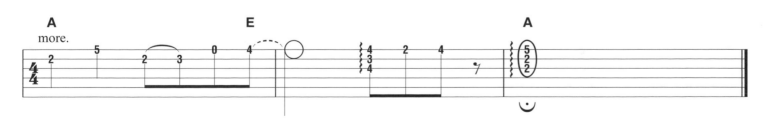

A   E   A

more.

La Bamba

By Ritchie Valens

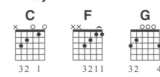

Key of C
Intro
Moderately fast

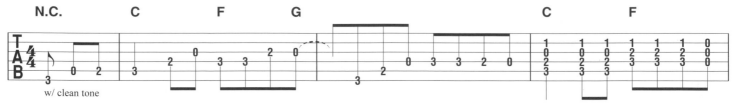

w/ clean tone

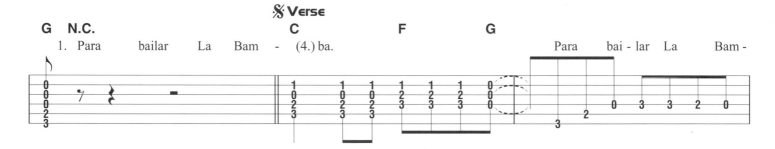

% **Verse**

1. Para bailar La Bam - (4.) ba. Para bai - lar La Bam -

C		F	G		C		F	G
etc.								
- ba se ne - ce - si	- ta una	poca de	gracia.		Una poca de		

C		F	G		C		F	G
gracia,	para mí para ti	y arriba,	y arri -	ba.		Y arriba,	y arri -	

To Coda ⊕

C		F	G		C		F	G N.C.
- ba, por ti seré,		por ti se -	ré, por ti seré.		2. Yo no soy mari -			

Verse

C		F	G		C		F	G
nero,		Yo no soy mari	- nero, soy cap - i - tán,		soy cap i - tán,			

Chorus

C		F	G		C		F	G
soy cap - i - tán.			Bam - ba, Bam	- ba.				

C		F	G		C		F	G
Bam - ba, Bam	- ba.			Bam - ba, Bam	- ba.			

Verse

C	F	G	N.C.		C	F	G

| Bam. | | | | 3. Para bailar la bam | - ba. | | Para bailar La Bam- |

C	F	G		C	F	G

| - ba se ne - ce - si | - ta una poca de | gracia. | | Una poca de |

Guitar Solo

C	F	G		C	F	G

| gracia, para mí para ti | y arriba, y arri | - ba. | | ‖ |

D.S. al Coda

C	F	G		*Play 7 times* C N.C.

‖: | | | :‖ 4. Para bailar la bam - ‖

⊕ Coda

Outro

Repeat and fade

C	F	G

| ‖: Bam - ba, Bam | - ba. :‖ |

La Grange

Words and Music by Billy F Gibbons, Dusty Hill and Frank Lee Beard

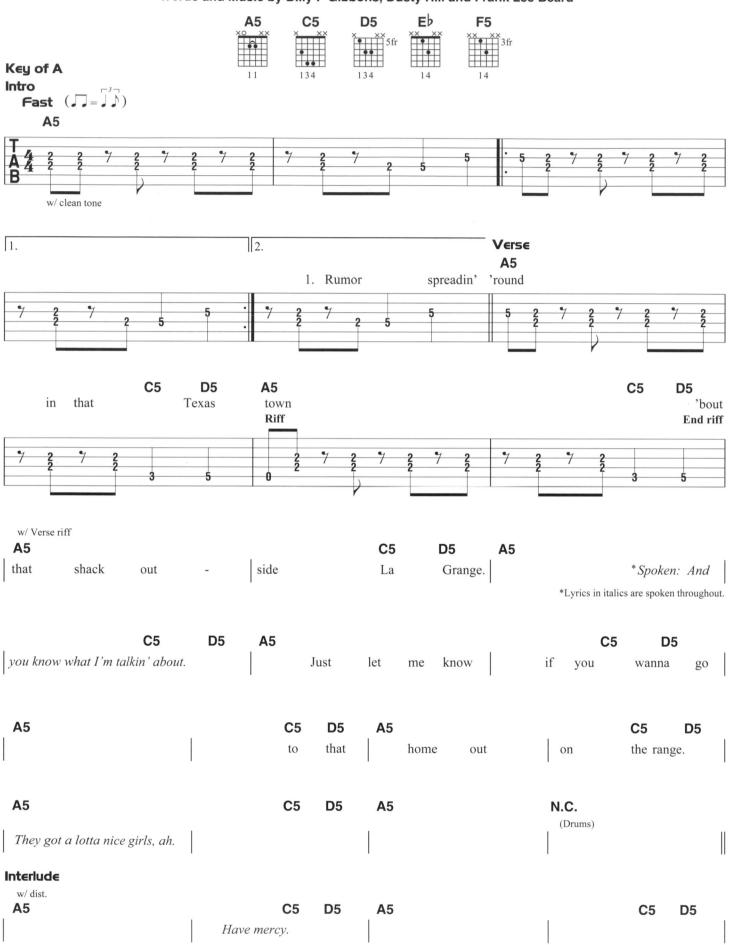

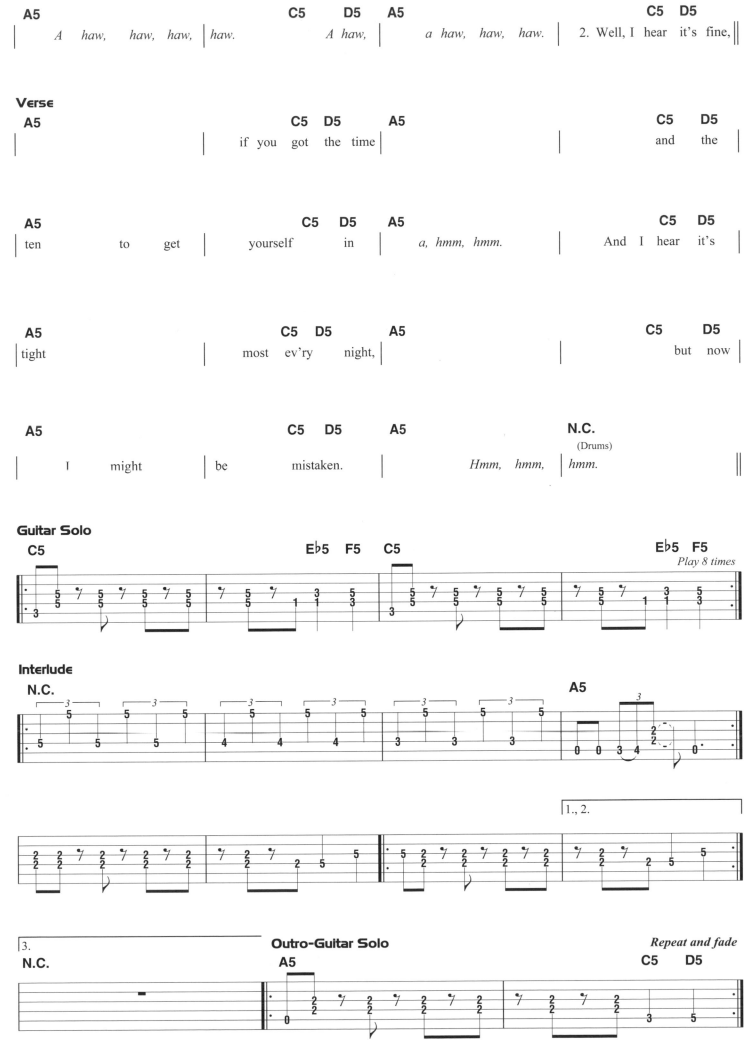

Lonely Boy

Words and Music by Dan Auerbach, Patrick Carney and Brian Burton

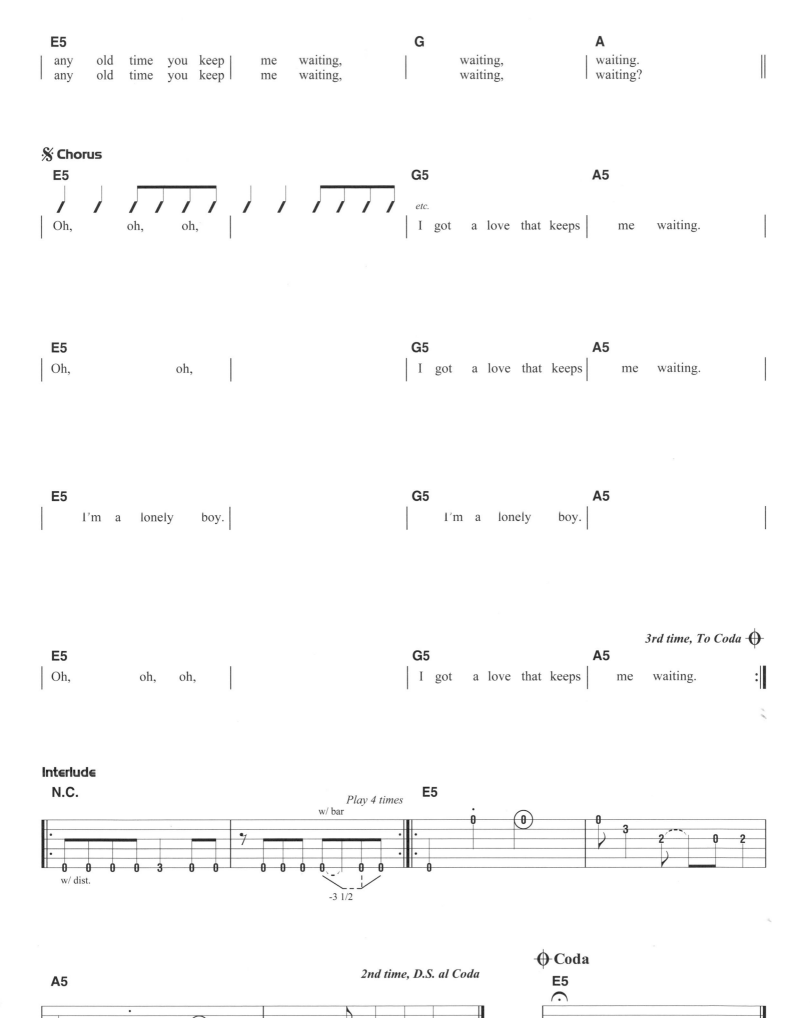

Love Story

Words and Music by Taylor Swift

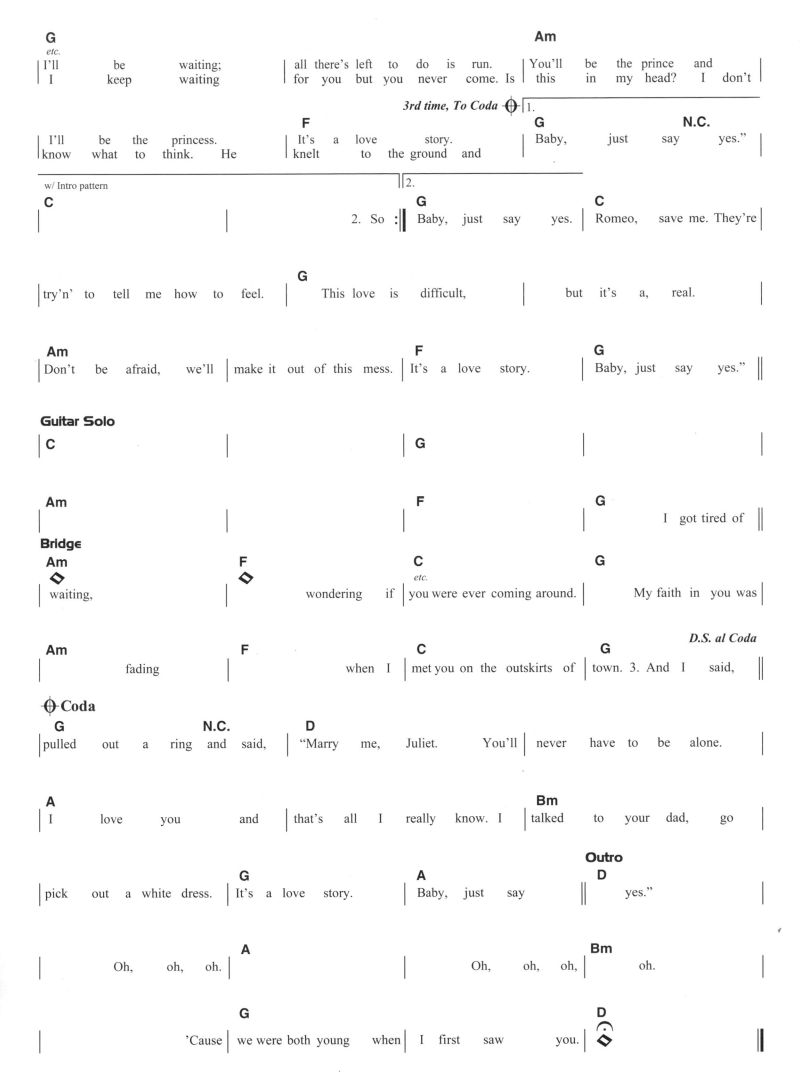

Man in the Box

Written by Jerry Cantrell, Layne Staley, Sean Kinney and Michael Starr

E7(no3rd) G5 E5 D5 A5

Tune down 1/2 step:
(low to high) Eb-Ab-Db-Gb-Bb-Eb

Key of Em

Intro

Moderately

E7(no3rd)

Ah, ah, ah, ah, ah, ah, ah, ah, ah.

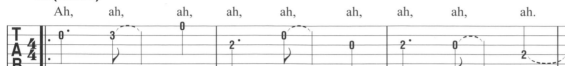

w/ dist.

Ah, ah, ah, ah, ah, ah, ah, ah, ah.

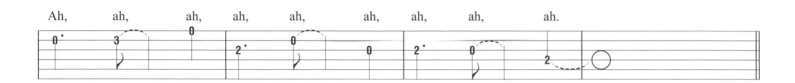

𝄋 Verse

E7(no3rd)

1. I'm the man in the box.
2. I'm the dog who gets beat.

3rd time, Guitar solo

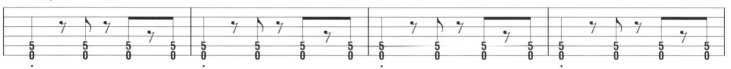

Bur - ied in my shit.
Shove my nose in shit.

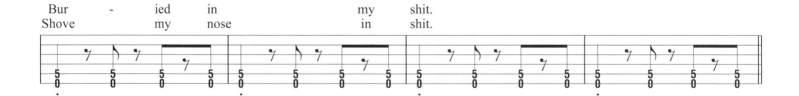

Pre-Chorus

G5

Won't you come and save

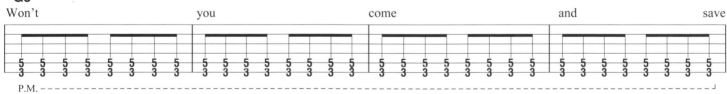

P.M. -

E7(no3rd)

me? Save me.

Guitar solo ends

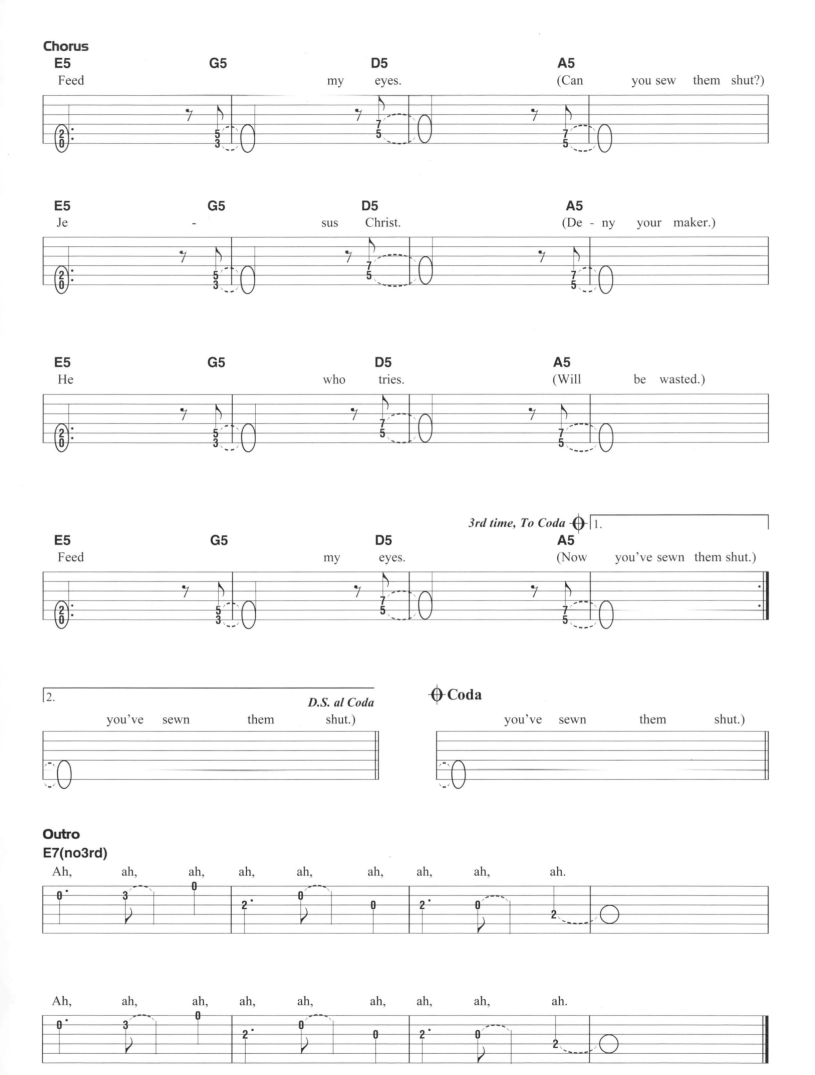

Old Time Rock & Roll

Words and Music by George Jackson and Thomas E. Jones III

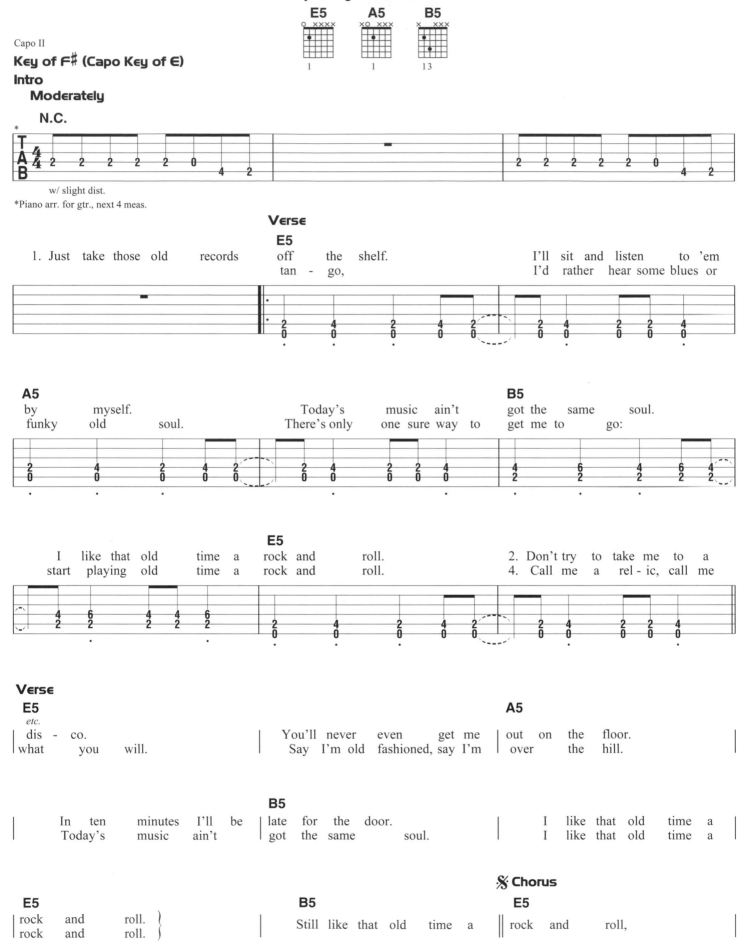

A5

| that kind of music just | soothes the soul. | I reminisce about the |

3rd time, To Coda ⊕

B5   **E5**   **B5**

| days of old | with that old time a | rock and roll. | ‖

Solo

E5 | | **A5** | | **B5** | |

                                              1.   **2.**

                E5   **B5**   **B5**   *D.S. al Coda*

| | | 3. Won't go to hear 'em play a ‖: Still like that old time a ‖

⊕ **Coda**   **Breakdown-Chorus**

B5   **N.C.**

| Still like that old time a ‖ rock and roll, | that kind of music just |

| soothes the soul. | I reminisce about the | days of old | |

| with that old time a | rock and roll. Hey! | **B5** Still like that old time a ‖

Outro-Chorus

E5   **A5**

‖: rock and roll,
 : rock and roll. *Instrumental* | that kind of music just | soothes the soul. |

B5

| I reminisce about the | days of old | with that old time a |

Repeat and fade

E5   **B5**

| rock and roll. | Still like that old time a :‖

Otherside

Words and Music by Anthony Kiedis, Flea, John Frusciante and Chad Smith

Key of Am
Intro
Moderately

w/ clean tone

*Bass & gtr. arr. for gtr., next 4 meas.

𝄋 Chorus

w/ Intro riff

Am How long, how **F** long will I **C** slide, **G** sep - ar - ate my

Am side? **F** I don't, **C** I **G** don't be - lieve it's

Am bad; **F** **C** slittin' my throat, it's all **G** I ev - er...

3rd time, To Coda ⊕

Verse

Am 1. I heard your voice through a **Em** photograph. **Am** I thought it up, it brought
3. Pour my life into a paper cup; the ashtray's full and I'm

etc.

Em up the past. **Am** Once you know you can **Em** never go back. } I've got to
spil - lin' my guts. She wants to know am I still a slut.

G take it on the **A** other side.

Verse

w/ Verse riff

Am 2. Centuries are what it **Em** meant to me; **Am** a cemetery where I
4. Scarlet starlet and she's in my bed, a candidate a, for my

Em marry the sea. **Am** Stranger things could never **Em** change my mind. } I've got to
soul mate bled. Push the trigger and pull the thread.

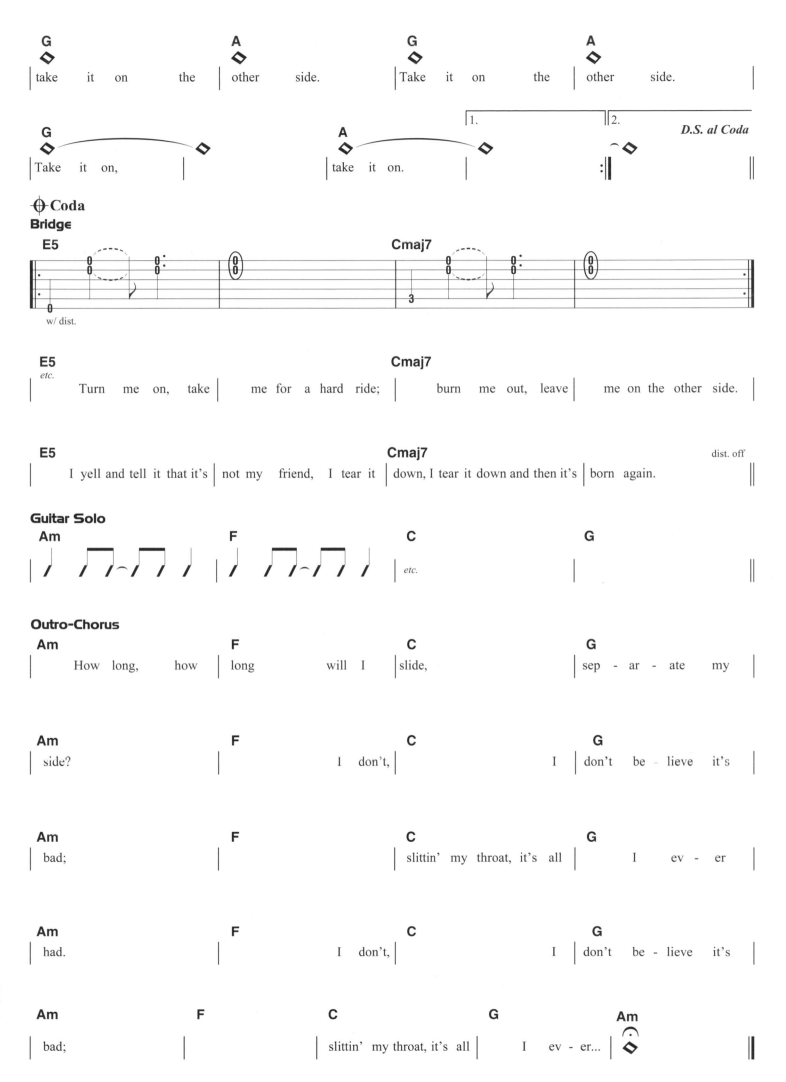

G   A   G   A

take it on the | other side. | Take it on the | other side. |

1.   2.   *D.S. al Coda*

G   A

Take it on, | | take it on. | | :|| ||

Coda
Bridge

E5   **Cmaj7**

w/ dist.

E5   **Cmaj7**

etc.   Turn me on, take | me for a hard ride; | burn me out, leave | me on the other side. |

E5   **Cmaj7**   dist. off

I yell and tell it that it's | not my friend, I tear it | down, I tear it down and then it's | born again. ||

Guitar Solo

Am   **F**   **C**   **G**

etc.

Outro-Chorus

Am   **F**   **C**   **G**

How long, how | long will I | slide, | sep - ar - ate my |

Am   **F**   **C**   **G**

side? | | I don't, | I | don't be - lieve it's |

Am   **F**   **C**   **G**

bad; | | slittin' my throat, it's all | I ev - er |

Am   **F**   **C**   **G**

had. | | I don't, | I | don't be - lieve it's |

Am   **F**   **C**   **G**   **Am**

bad; | | slittin' my throat, it's all | I ev - er... | ||

Pork and Beans

Words and Music by Rivers Cuomo

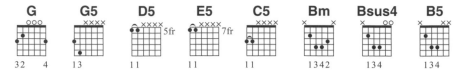

G G5 D5 E5 C5 Bm Bsus4 B5

Tune down 1/2 step:
(low to high) Eb-Ab-Db-Gb-Bb-Eb

Key of G

Intro

Moderately

G

w/ clean tone

etc.

| - gaine | to | put in | my | hair. |
| to | a | happy | | song |

| Work it | out | at | the gym | to | fit my | underwear. |
| catchy | chorus | and beat | so | they can sing | along. |

Verse

G

1. They say I need some Ro -
2. Ev'ryone likes to dance

with a

| Oakley | makes | the | shades | to transform | a | tool. |
| Timbaland | knows | the | way | to reach the top | of | the chart. |

| You'd | hate for | the kids | to | think |
| Maybe | if | I work | with | him |

| that you | lost | your | cool. |
| I can | perfect | the | art. |

I'm a

G5

w/ dist.

𝄋 Chorus

G5
do the things that I

D5
wanna do,

E5
I ain't got a thing to

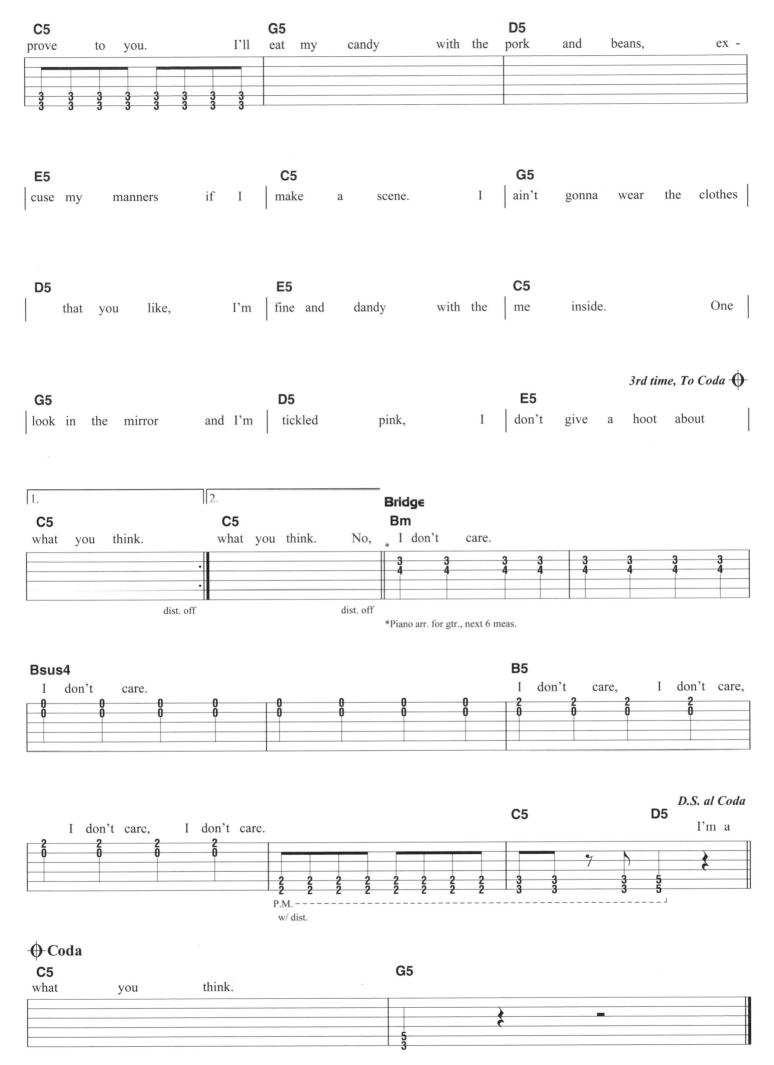

Rock and Roll

Words and Music by Jimmy Page, Robert Plant, John Paul Jones and John Bonham

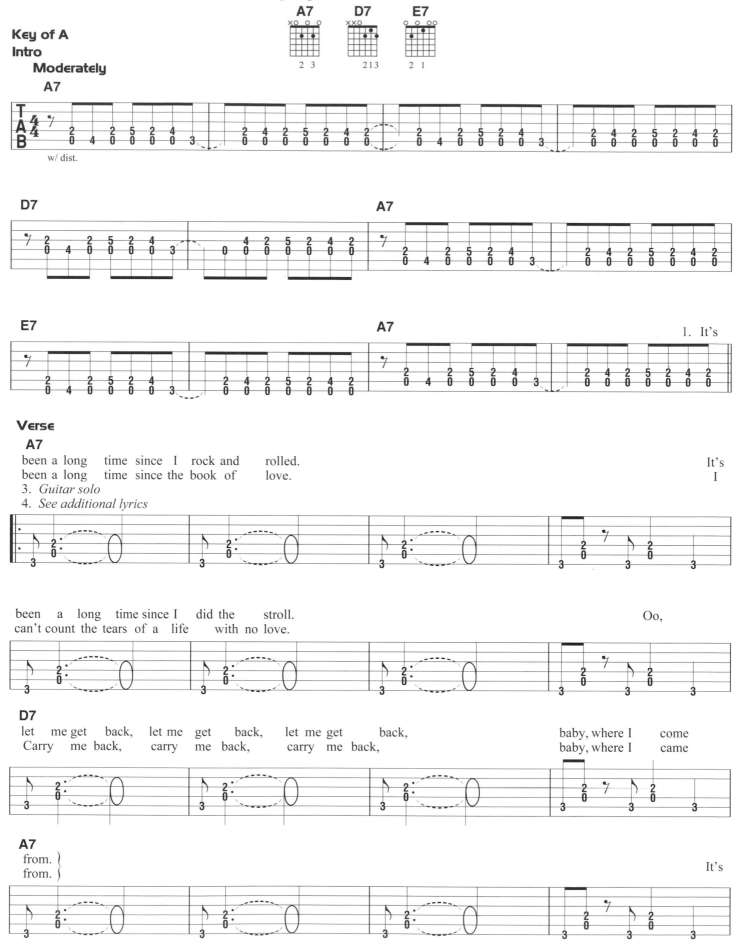

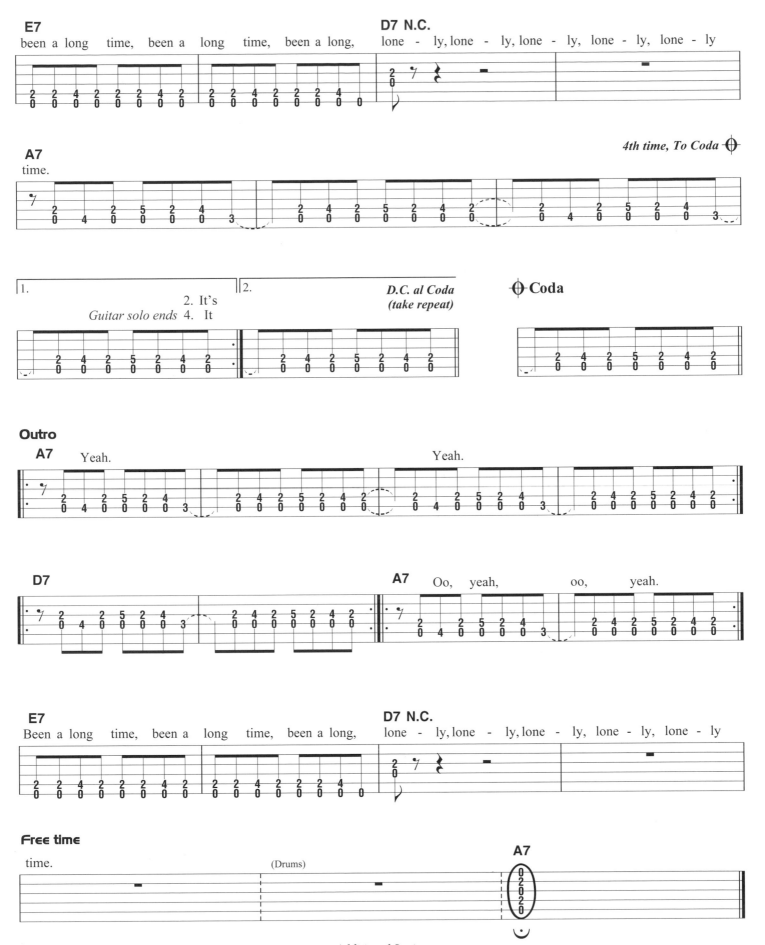

Additional Lyrics

4. It seems so long since we walked in the moonlight,
   Making vows that just couldn't work right.
   Open your arms, open your arms, open your arms,
   Baby, let my love come running in.
   It's been a long time, been a long time, been a long,
   Lonely, lonely, lonely, lonely, lonely time.

Rolling in the Deep

Words and Music by Adele Adkins and Paul Epworth

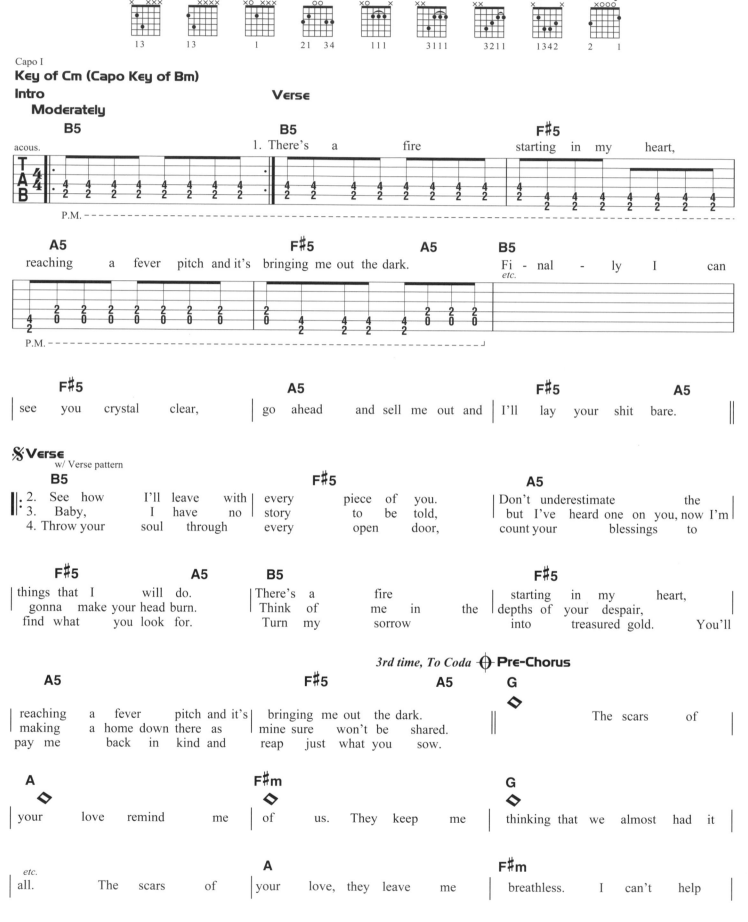

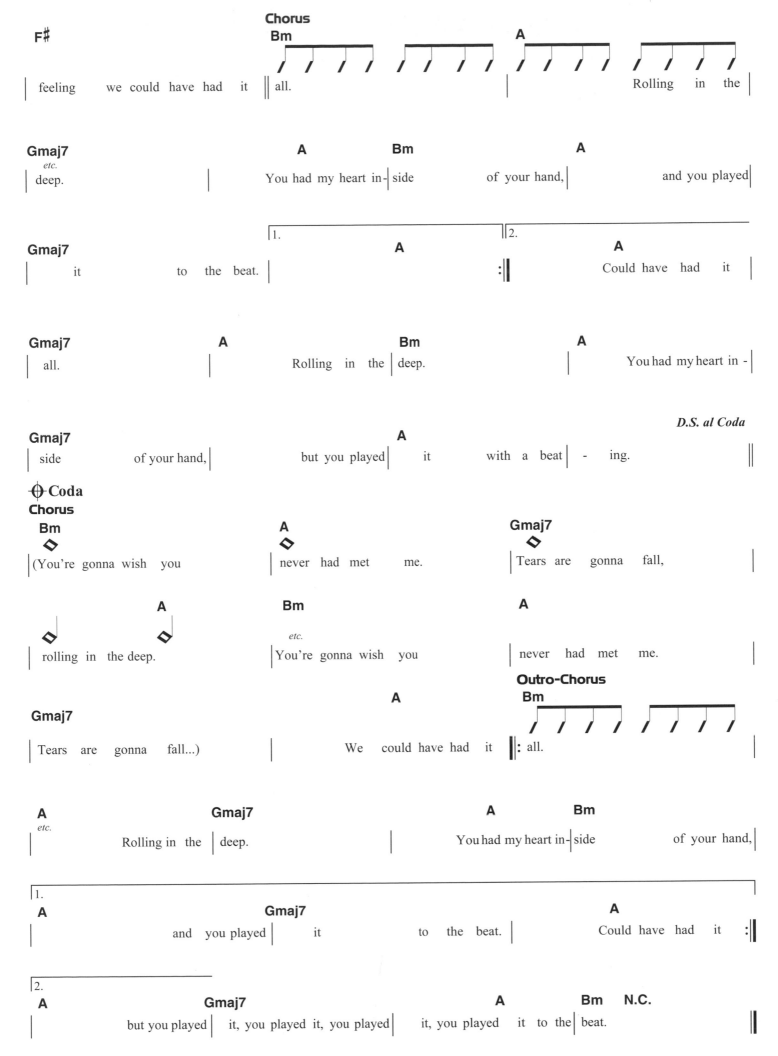

Scarborough Fair/Canticle

Arrangement and Original Counter Melody by Paul Simon and Arthur Garfunkel

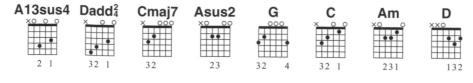

A13sus4 Dadd$^2_4$ Cmaj7 Asus2 G C Am D

Capo VII

Key of Em (Capo Key of Am)

Intro

Moderately fast

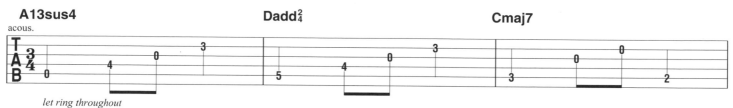

let ring throughout

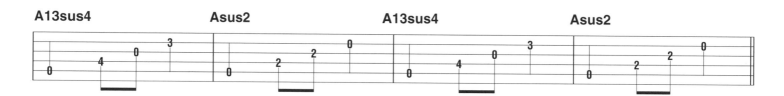

Verse

A13sus4   Asus2   G

1., 5. Are   you   goin'   to   Scarborough

2., 3., 4. *See additional lyrics*

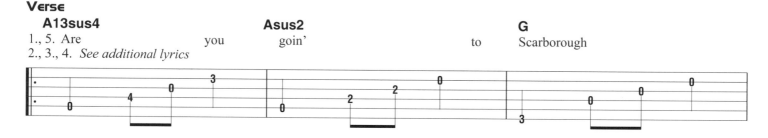

A13sus4   Asus2   C

Fair?   Parsley,

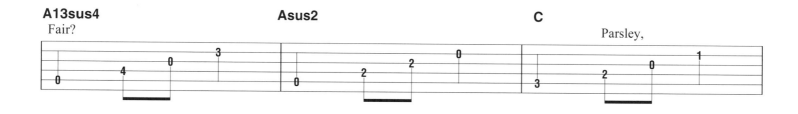

Am   C   D   A13sus4

sage,   rose - mary   and   thyme.

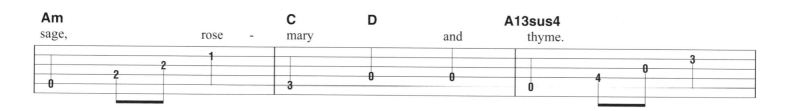

Asus2   A13sus4   Asus2

Re -

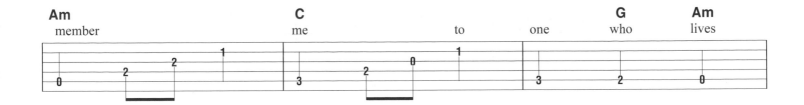
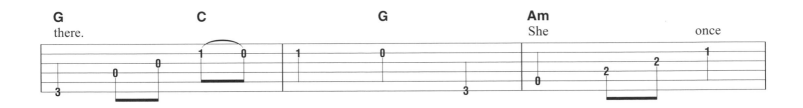
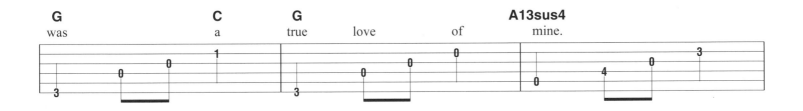
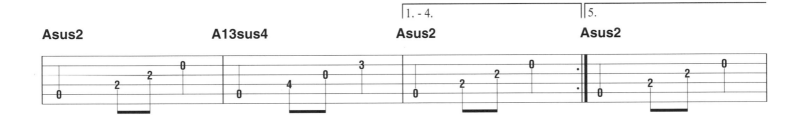
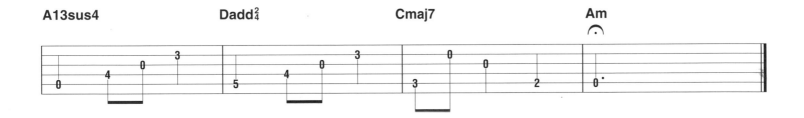

Additional Lyrics

2. Tell her to make me a cambric shirt.
   (On the side of a hill in the deep forest green.)
   Parsley, sage, rosemary and thyme.
   (Tracing of sparrow on snow-crested ground.)
   Without no seam nor needlework,
   (Blankets and bedclothes, the child of the mountain...)
   Then she'll be a true of love of mine.
   (...Sleeps unaware of the clarion call.)

3. Tell her to find me an acre of land.
   (On the side of a hill, a sprinkling of leaves...)
   Parsley, sage, rosemary and thyme.
   (...Washes the grave with so many tears.)
   Between the salt water and the sea strand,
   (A soldier cleans and polishes a gun.)
   Then she'll be a true love of mine.

4. Tell her to reap it in a sickle of leather.
   (War bellows blazing in scarlet battalions.)
   Parsley, sage, rosemary and thyme.
   (Generals order their soldiers to kill...)
   And gather it all in a bunch of heather,
   (...And to fight for a cause they've long ago forgotten.)
   Then she'll be a true love of mine.

Seven Nation Army

Words and Music by Jack White

Key of E
Intro
Moderately

w/ slight dist.

1. I'm gonna
2. Don't wanna
3. I'm going to

Verse
w/ Intro riff

N.C.

fight 'em off,		a seven nation	army couldn't hold me back.
hear about it,		ev'ry single	one's got a story to
Wichita,		far from this opera	forevermore.

tell.	They're gonna	rip it off,	taking their
	Ev'ryone	knows about it	from the Queen of
	I'm gonna	work the straw,	make the sweat

time right behind my back.		And I'm	talking to myself at night
England to the hounds of hell.		And if I	catch it coming back my way
drip out of ev'ry pore.		And I'm	bleeding, and I'm bleeding, and I'm

because I can't forget			And
I'm gonna serve it to you.			All the
bleeding right before the Lord.			

Back and forth through my mind	behind a cigarette.	
that ain't what you want to hear,	but that's what I'll do.	
words are gonna bleed from me	and I will think no more.	

And the   message coming from   my   eyes   says   leave it   alone.
And the   feeling coming from   my   bones   says   find   a   home.
And the   stains   coming from   my   blood   tell   me go back home.

Interlude

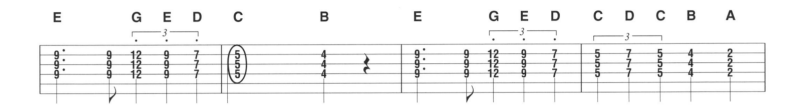

*Optional: w/ slide worn on pinky, next 8 meas.

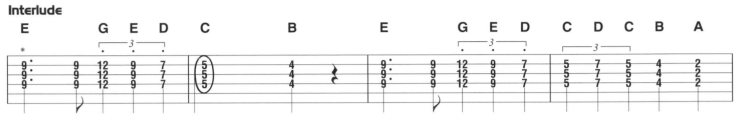

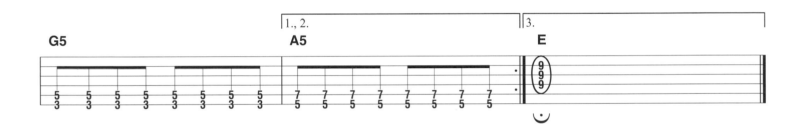

Smells Like Teen Spirit

Words and Music by Kurt Cobain, Krist Novoselic and Dave Grohl

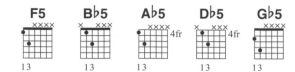

Key of Fm

Intro

Moderately

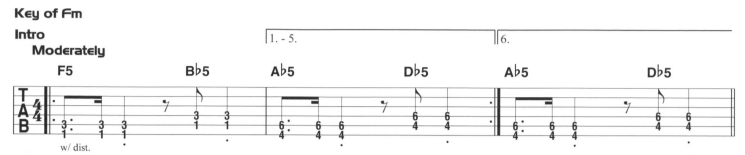

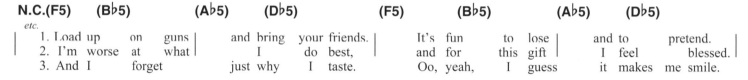

w/ clean tone

*Chords implied by bass.

Verse

N.C.(F5) (Bb5) (Ab5) (Db5) (F5) (Bb5) (Ab5) (Db5)

etc.
1. Load up on guns and bring your friends. It's fun to lose and to pretend.
2. I'm worse at what I do best, and for this gift I feel blessed.
3. And I forget just why I taste. Oo, yeah, I guess it makes me smile.

(F5) (Bb5) (Ab5) (Db5) (F5) (Bb5) (Ab5) (Db5)

She's o - ver - board and self - assured. Oh, no, I know a dirty word.
Our lit - tle group has al - ways been and al - ways will until the end.
I found it hard, it's hard to find. Oh well, what ev - er, never mind.

Pre-Chorus

N.C.(F5) (Bb5) (Ab5) (Db5) (F5) (Bb5) (Ab5) (Db5)

Hello, hello, hello, how low? Hello, hello, hello, how low?

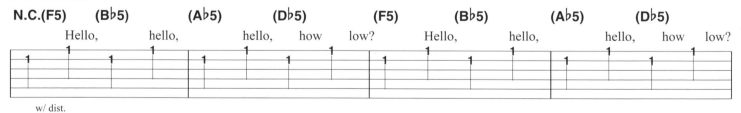

w/ dist.

(F5) (Bb5) (Ab5) (Db5) (F5) (Bb5) (Ab5) (Db5)

etc.
Hello, hello, hello, how low? Hello, hello, hello. With the lights

Chorus

F5	Bb5	Ab5	Db5	F5	Bb5	Ab5	Db5
out,	it's less dan - g'rous.		Here we are now,		entertain us.		I feel stu-

F5	Bb5	Ab5	Db5	F5	Bb5	Ab5	Db5
- pid and conta	- gious.	Here we are	now,	entertain	us.	A mulat -	

3rd time, To Coda ⊕

F5	Bb5	Ab5	Db5	F5	Bb5	Ab5	Db5
- to, an albi	- no,	a mosqui	- to,	my libi	- do.	Yeah.	

Bridge

2nd time, D.S. al Coda

F5	Gb5	N.C.	F5	Bb5 Ab5	F5	Gb5	N.C.	F5	Bb5 Ab5
	Yay.						Yay.		

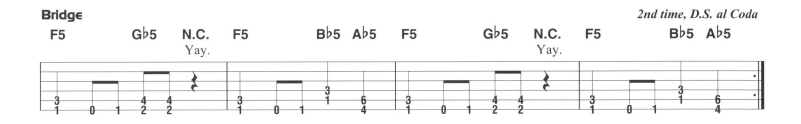

⊕ **Coda**

Outro

Ab5	Db5	F5	Bb5	Ab5	Db5	F5	Bb5
- do,	a deni	‖: - al,	a deni	- al,	a deni	- al,	a deni -

1.

Ab5	Db5		**2.** Ab5	Db5	F5
- al,	a deni -:‖		- al,	a deni	- al.

73

Smoke on the Water

Words and Music by Ritchie Blackmore, Ian Gillan, Roger Glover, Jon Lord and Ian Paice

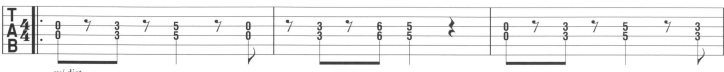

Key of Gm
Intro
   Moderately
     N.C.(G5)

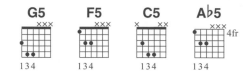

w/ dist.

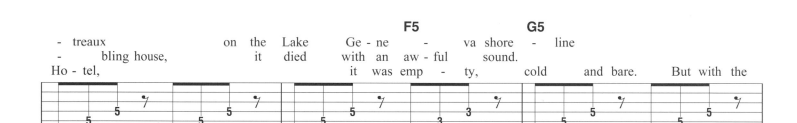

1. We all came out to Mon-
2. They burned down the gam-
3. We end-ed up at the Grand

- treaux on the Lake Ge-ne - va shore - line
- bling house, it died with an aw-ful sound.
Ho-tel, it was emp-ty, cold and bare. But with the

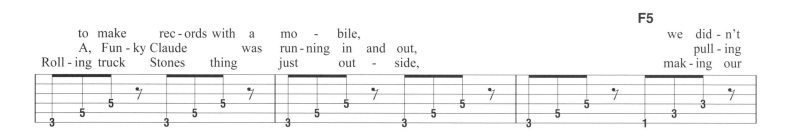

to make rec-ords with a mo - bile, we did-n't
A, Fun-ky Claude was run-ning in and out, pull-ing
Roll-ing truck Stones thing just out-side, mak-ing our

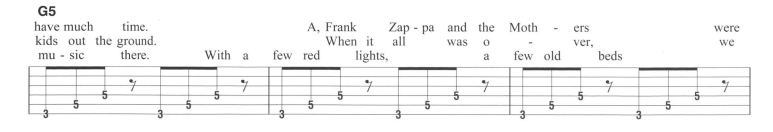

have much time. A, Frank Zap-pa and the Moth-ers were
kids out the ground. When it all was o - ver, we
mu-sic there. With a few red lights, a few old beds

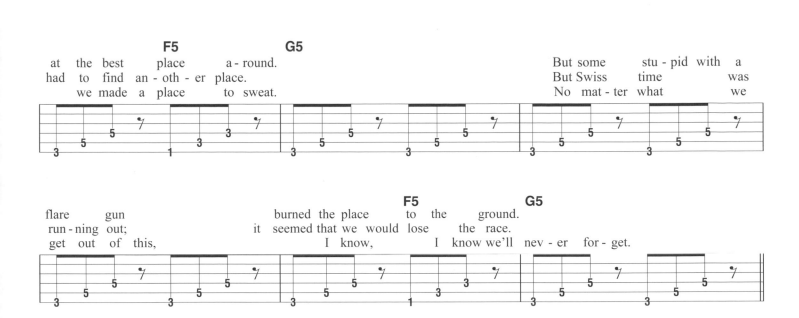

at the best place a - round.
had to find an - oth - er place.
we made a place to sweat.

But some stu - pid with a
But Swiss time was
No mat - ter what we

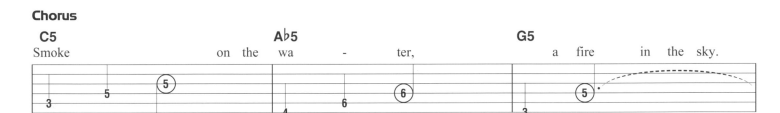

flare gun
run - ning out;
get out of this,

burned the place to the ground.
it seemed that we would lose the race.
I know, I know we'll nev - er for - get.

Chorus

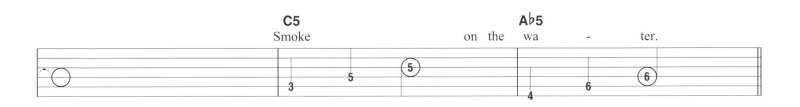

Smoke on the wa - ter, a fire in the sky.

Smoke on the wa - ter.

Interlude

N.C.(G5)

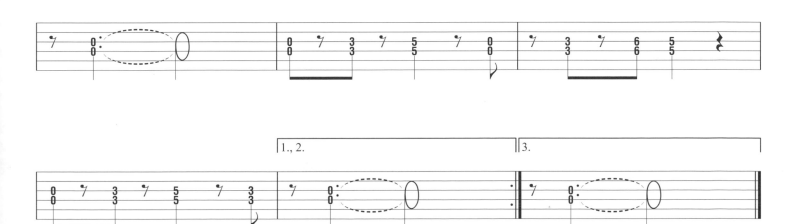

Sunday Bloody Sunday

Words and Music by U2

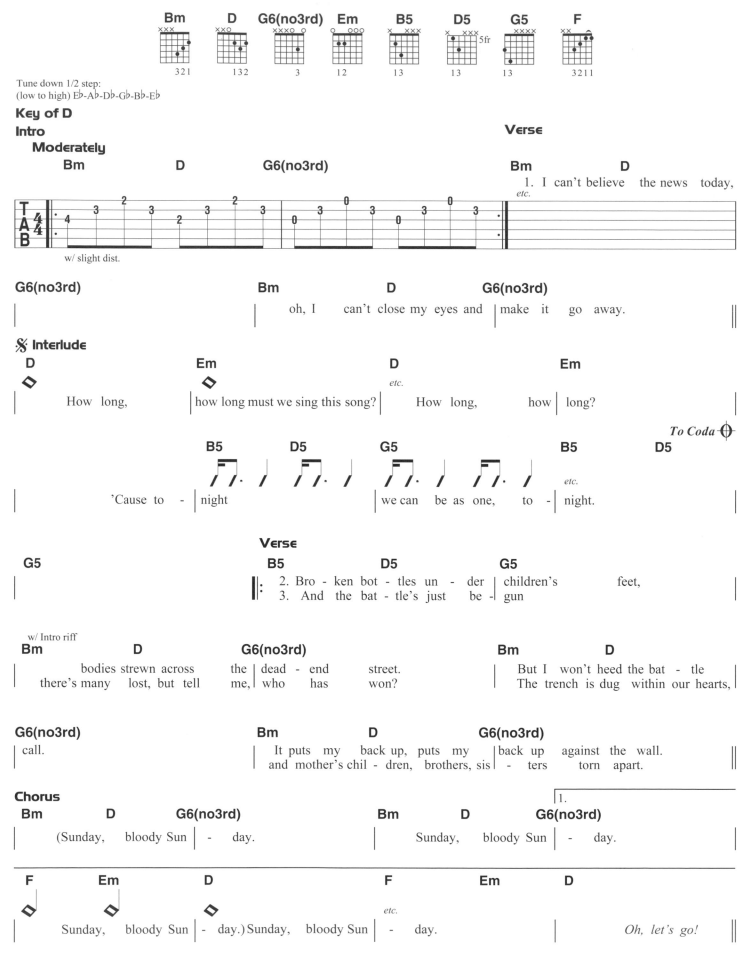

Tune down 1/2 step:
(low to high) Eb-Ab-Db-Gb-Bb-Eb

Key of D

Intro
Moderately

w/ slight dist.

Verse

1. I can't believe the news today, *etc.*

oh, I can't close my eyes and make it go away.

Interlude

How long, how long must we sing this song? *etc.* How long, how long?

To Coda

'Cause to - night we can be as one, to - night. *etc.*

Verse

2. Bro - ken bot - tles un - der children's feet,
3. And the bat - tle's just be - gun

w/ Intro riff

bodies strewn across the dead - end street. But I won't heed the bat - tle
there's many lost, but tell me, who has won? The trench is dug within our hearts,

call. It puts my back up, puts my back up against the wall.
and mother's chil - dren, brothers, sis - ters torn apart.

Chorus

1.

(Sunday, bloody Sun - day. Sunday, bloody Sun - day.

Sunday, bloody Sun - day.) Sunday, bloody Sun - day. *etc.* *Oh, let's go!*

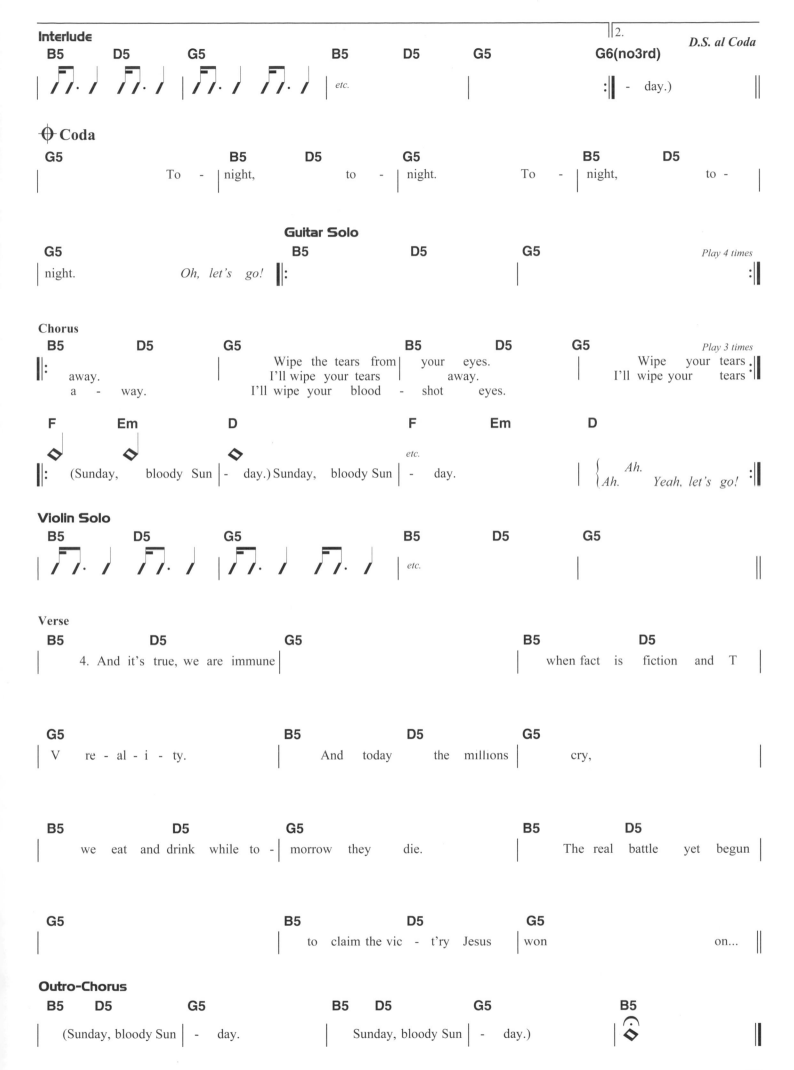

Susie-Q

Words and Music by Dale Hawkins, Stan Lewis and Eleanor Broadwater

Three Little Birds

Words and Music by Bob Marley

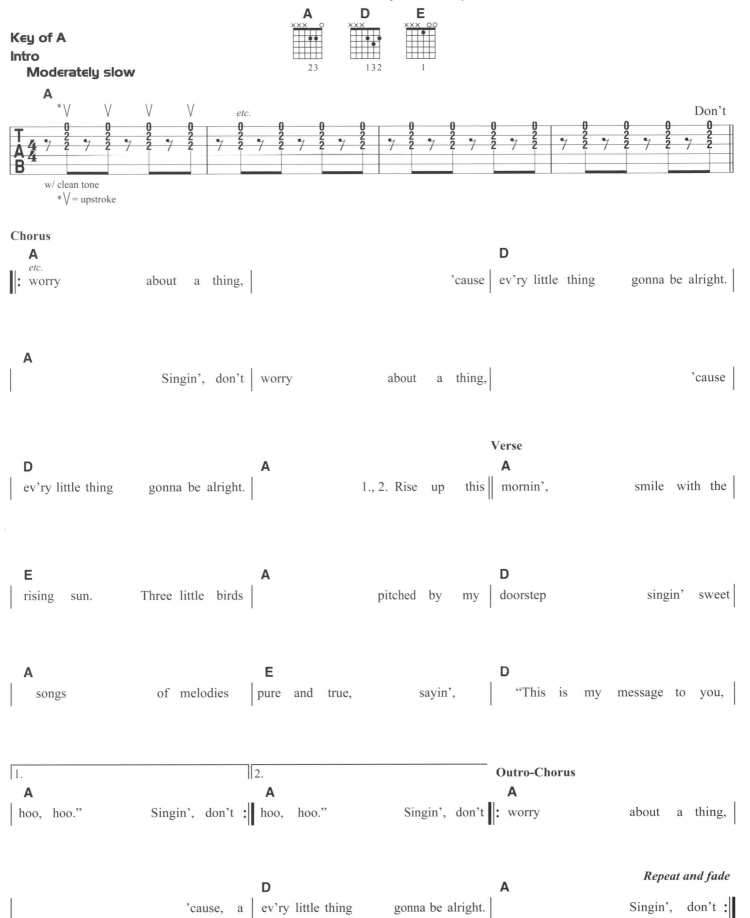

Sweet Home Chicago

Words and Music by Robert Johnson

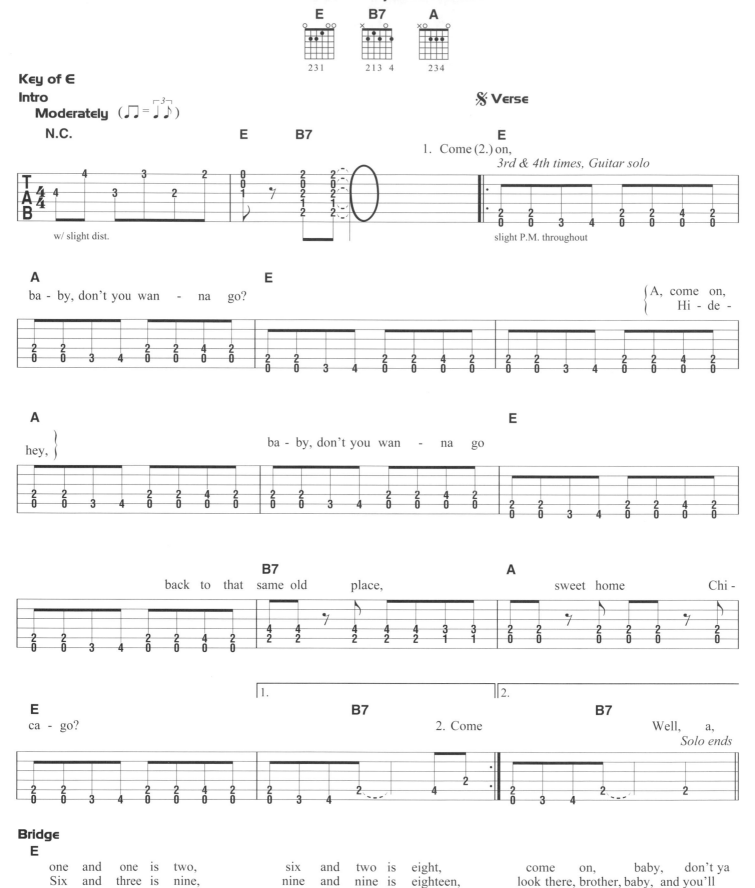

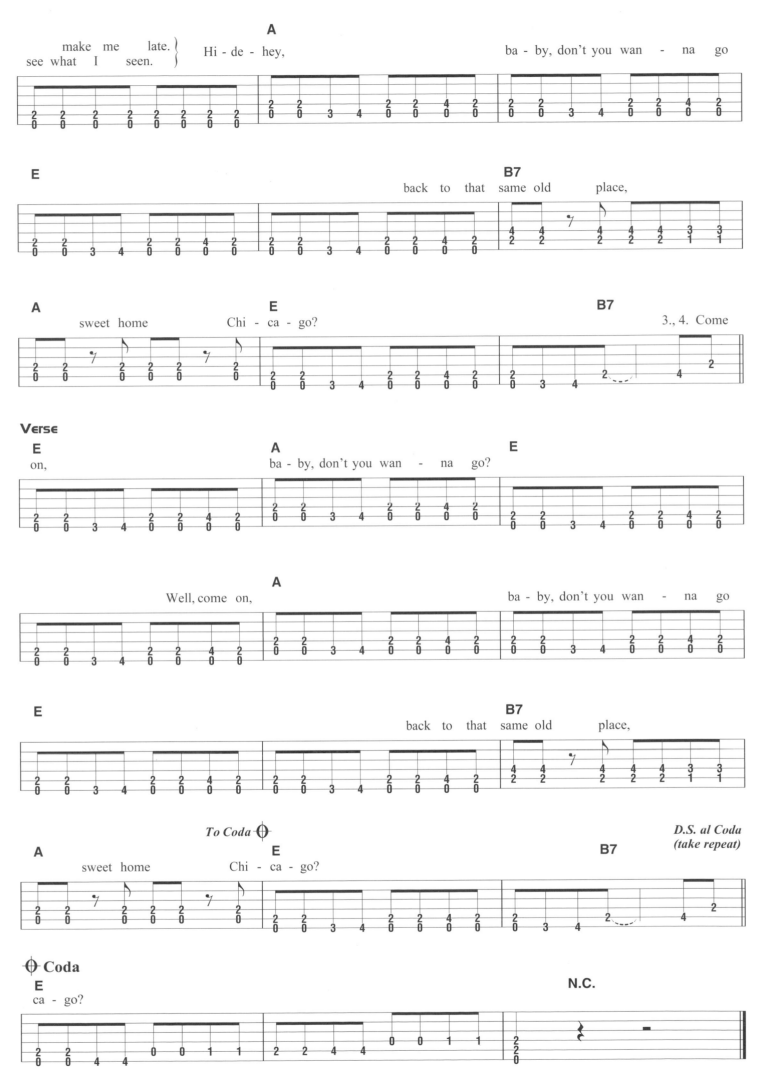

That'll Be the Day

Words and Music by Jerry Allison, Norman Petty and Buddy Holly

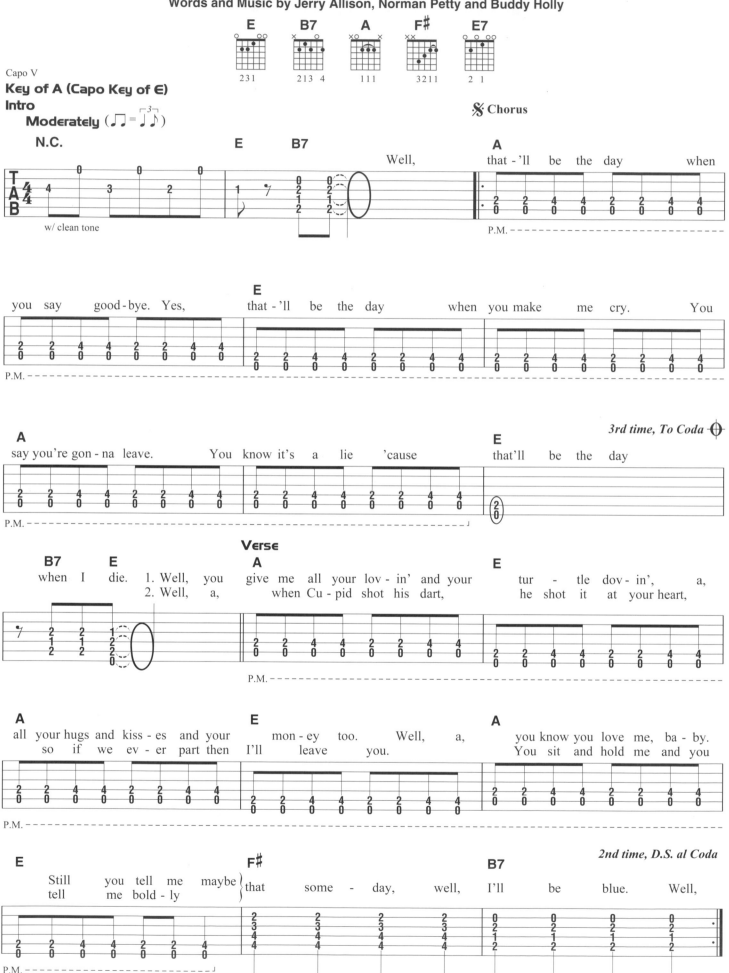

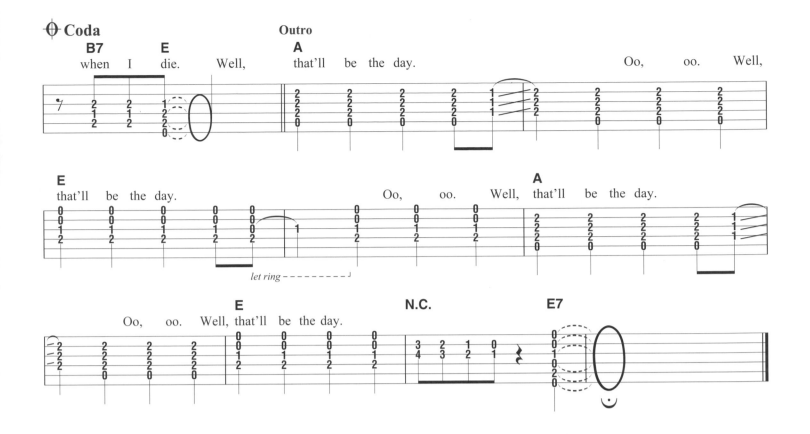

What I Got

Words and Music by Brad Nowell, Eric Wilson, Floyd Gaugh and Lindon Roberts

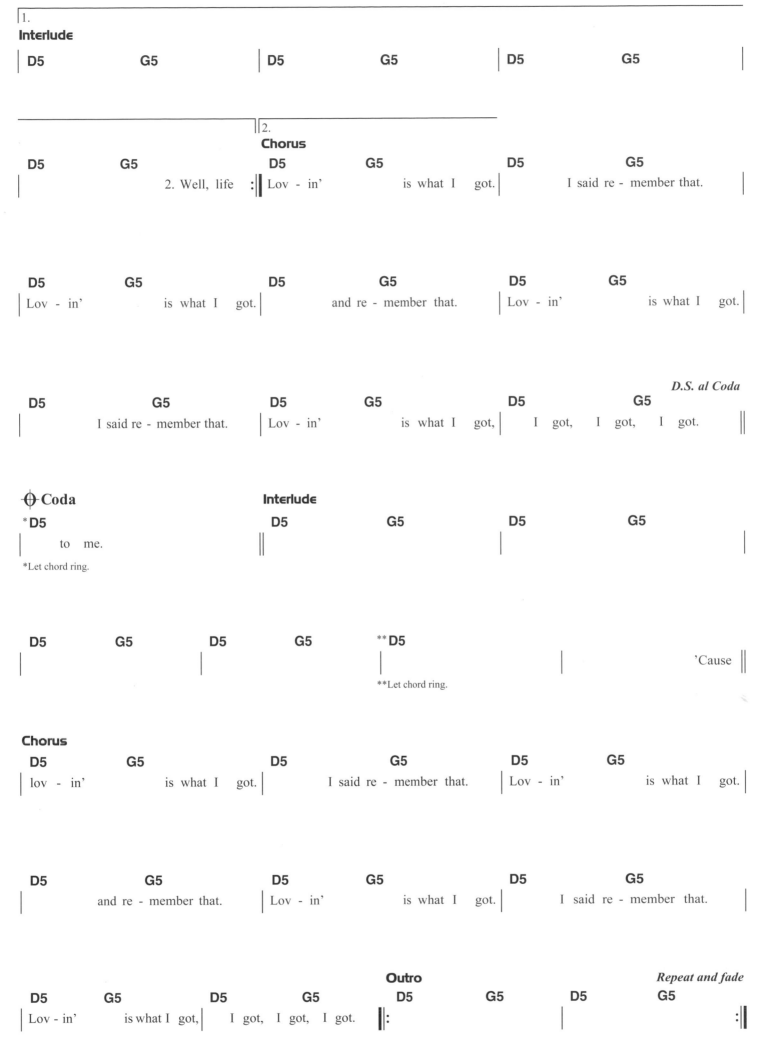

Wild Night

Words and Music by Van Morrison

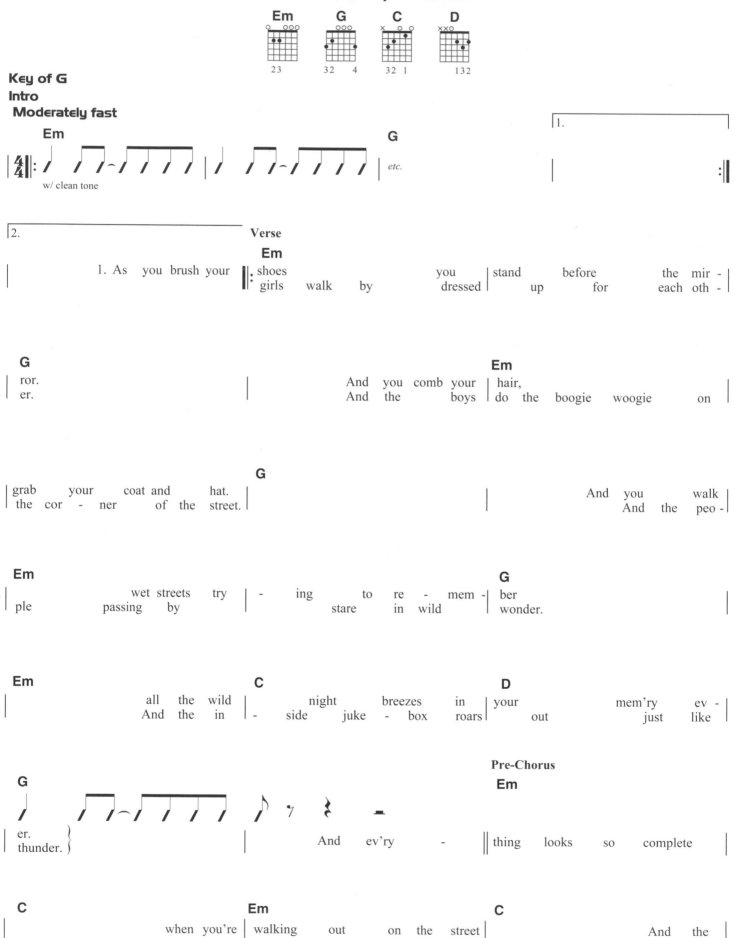

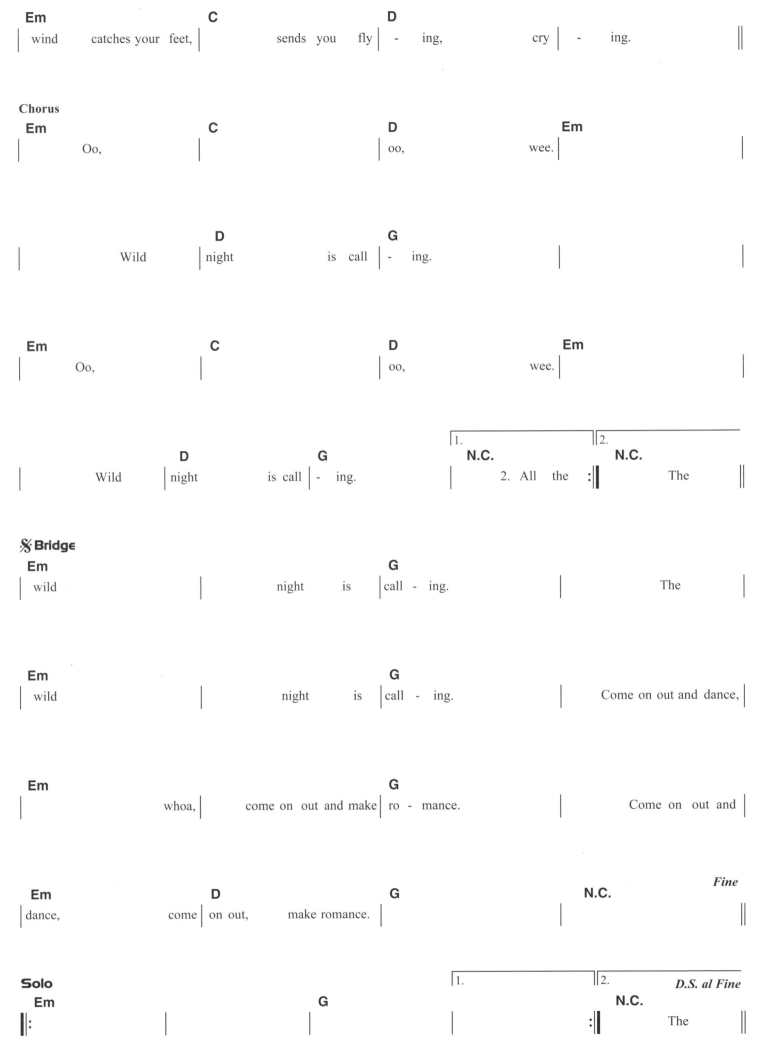

Em   **C**   **D**

| wind   catches your feet, | sends you fly | - ing,   cry | - ing. ‖

Chorus

Em   **C**   **D**   **Em**

| Oo, | oo,   wee. | | |

D   **G**

| Wild | night   is call | - ing. | |

Em   **C**   **D**   **Em**

| Oo, | oo,   wee. | |

1. N.C.   2. N.C.

D   **G**

| Wild | night   is call | - ing. | 2. All the :‖   The ‖

𝄋 Bridge

Em   **G**

| wild | night is | call - ing. | The |

Em   **G**

| wild | night is | call - ing. | Come on out and dance, |

Em   **G**

| whoa, | come on out and make | ro - mance. | Come on out and |

Fine

Em   **D**   **G**   **N.C.**

| dance, | come | on out,   make romance. | | ‖

Solo

1.   2.   *D.S. al Fine*

Em   **G**   **N.C.**

‖: | | | :‖   The ‖

Wild Thing

Words and Music by Chip Taylor

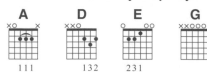

A   D   E   G

Key of A
Intro
    Moderately

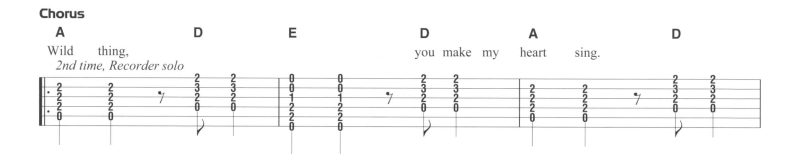

w/ slight dist.

Chorus

Wild   thing,   you make my heart sing.
2nd time, Recorder solo

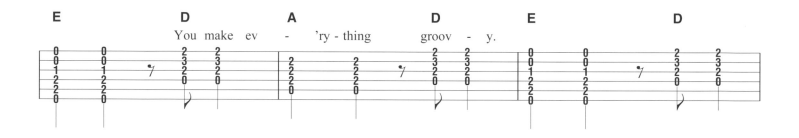

You make ev -   'ry - thing   groov - y.

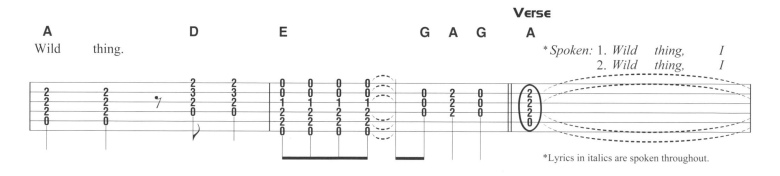

Verse

Wild   thing.   * Spoken: 1. Wild   thing,   I*
                                   2. Wild   thing,   I

*Lyrics in italics are spoken throughout.

think I love you,   but I wanna know   for sure.
think you move me,

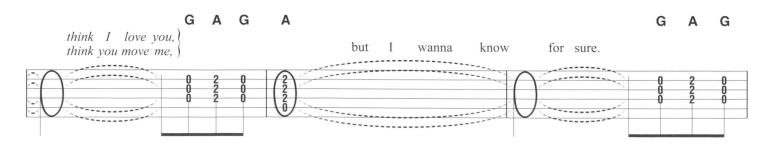

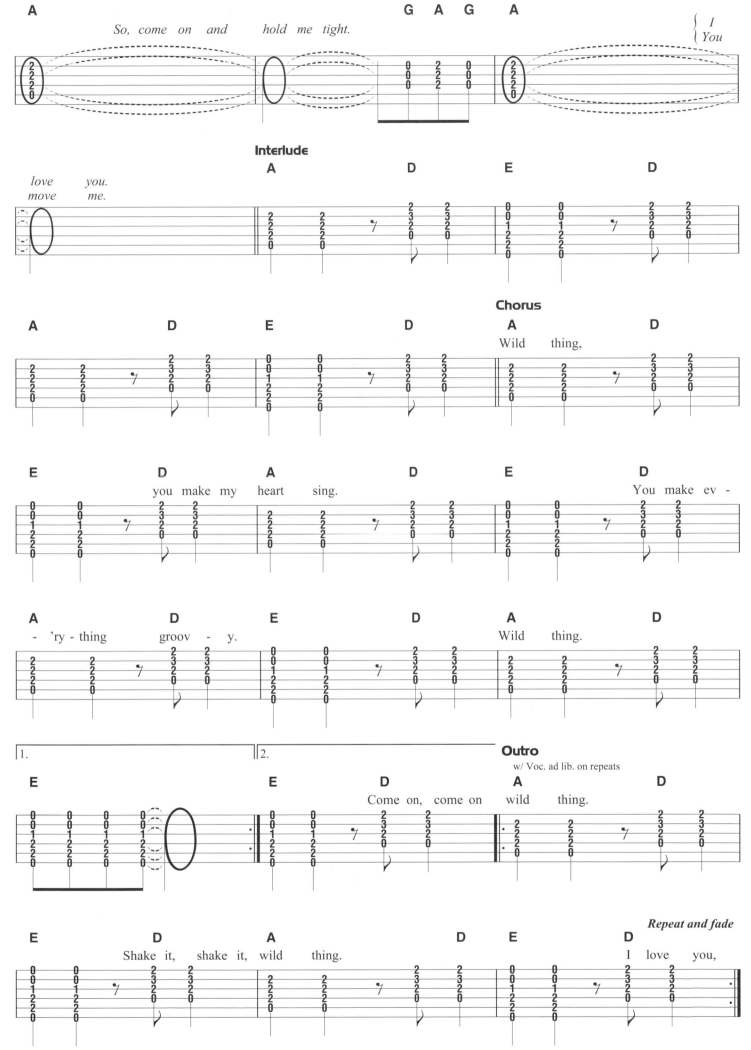

Wish You Were Here

Words and Music by Roger Waters and David Gilmour

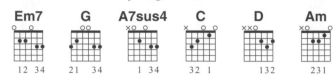

Key of G
Intro
Slow

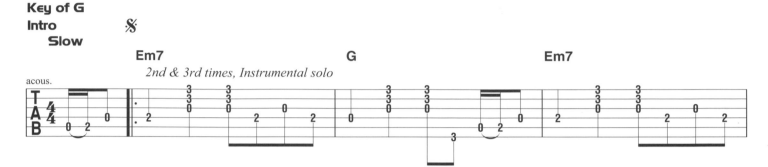

2nd & 3rd times, Instrumental solo

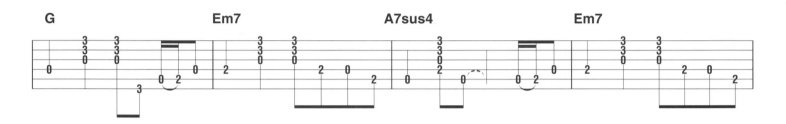

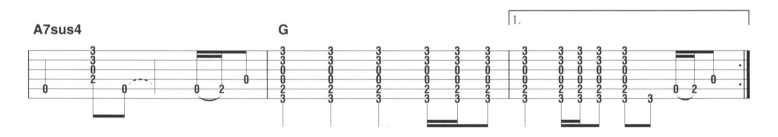

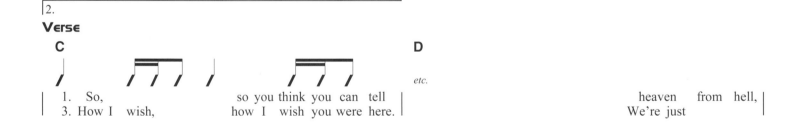

Verse

1. So,   so you think you can tell   heaven   from hell,
3. How I wish,   how I wish you were here.   We're just

two lost souls swimming in a   fish - bowl,   year after year.   Can you tell a green

field   from a cold   steel | rail,   a smile   from a veil?
Running over the same old ground,   what have we found?   The same old

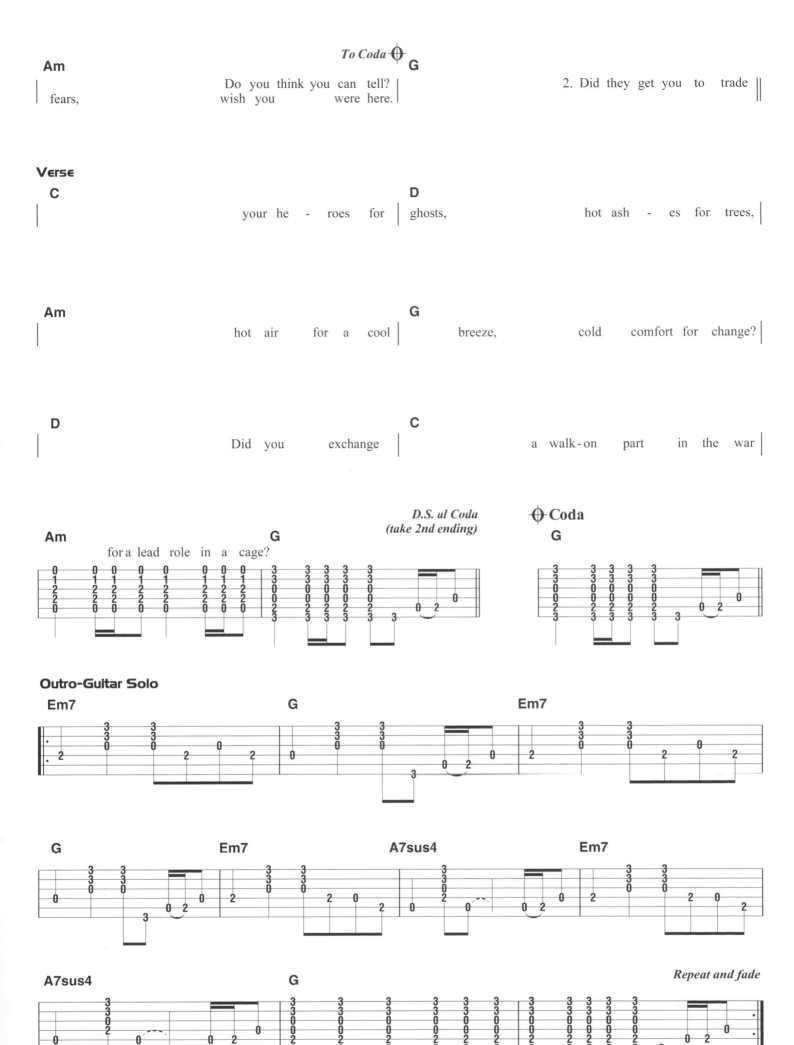

Verse

Outro-Guitar Solo

Repeat and fade

Wonderful Tonight

Words and Music by Eric Clapton

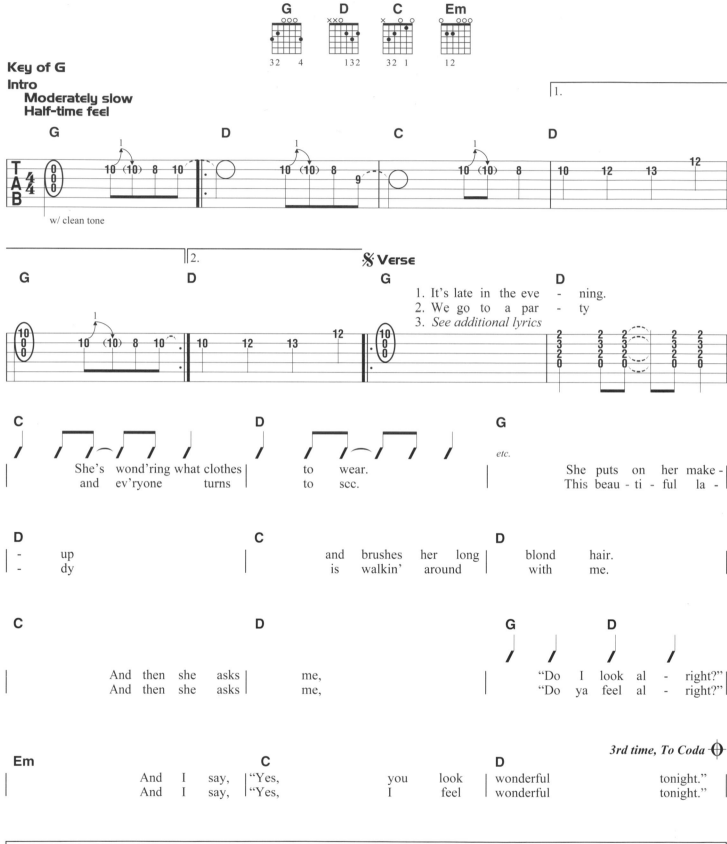

Key of G

Intro
 Moderately slow
 Half-time feel

w/ clean tone

Verse

1. It's late in the eve - ning.
2. We go to a par - ty
3. *See additional lyrics*

She's wond'ring what clothes to wear.
and ev'ryone turns to see.

etc.

She puts on her make -
This beau - ti - ful la -

- up and brushes her long blond hair.
- dy is walkin' around with me.

And then she asks me, "Do I look al - right?"
And then she asks me, "Do ya feel al - right?"

3rd time, To Coda

And I say, "Yes, you look wonderful tonight."
And I say, "Yes, I feel wonderful tonight."

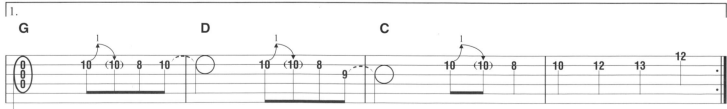

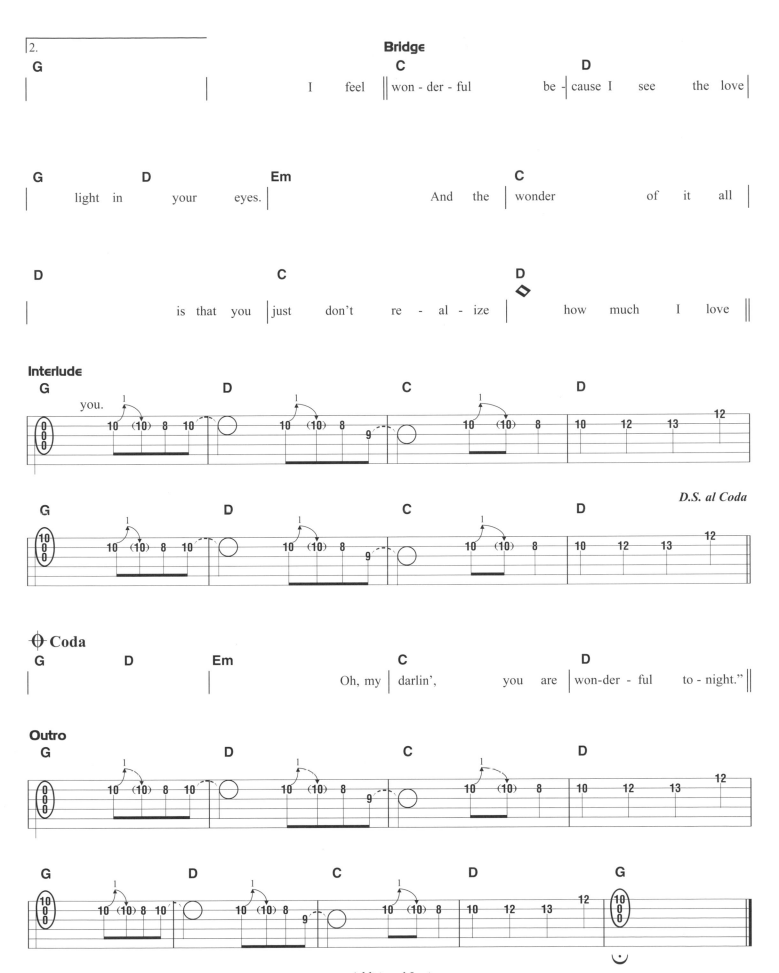

Additional Lyrics

3. It's time to go home now and I've got an aching head.
So I give her the car keys and she helps me to bed.
And then I tell her, as I turn out the light,
I say, "My darlin', you are wonderful tonight.
Oh, my darlin', you are wonderful tonight."

Wonderwall

Words and Music by Noel Gallagher

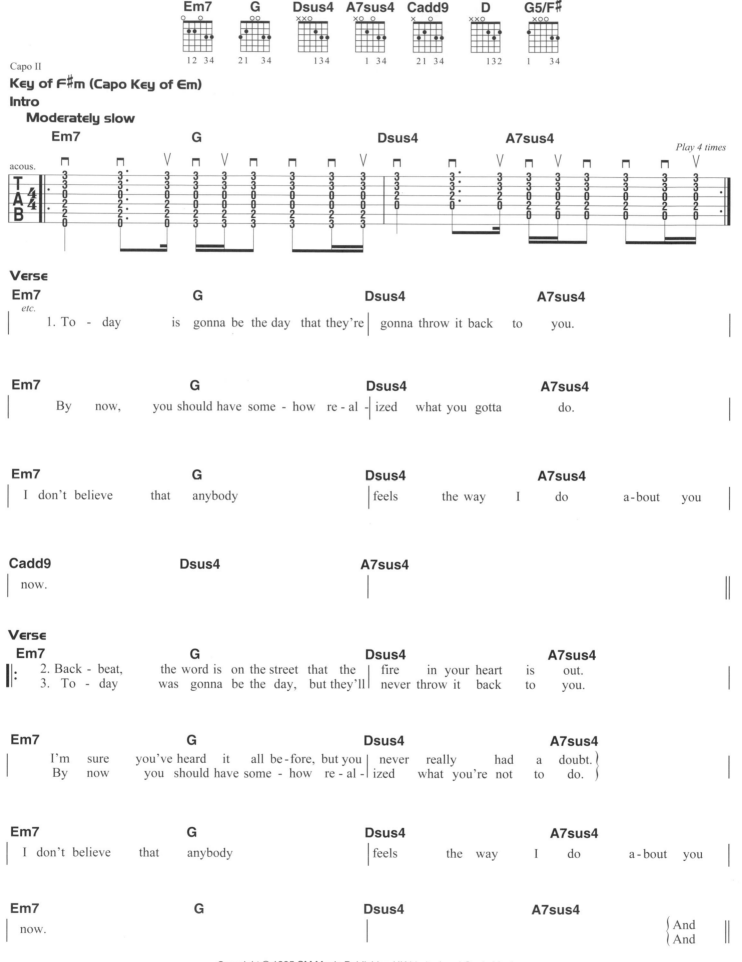

Pre-Chorus

Cadd9   D   Em7

| all the roads we have to walk are | winding,   and |
| all the roads that lead you there were | winding,   and |

Cadd9   D   Em7

| all the lights that lead us there are | blinding. }
| all the lights that light the way are | blinding. }

Cadd9   D   G   G5/F♯   Em7   G

| There are many things that I would | like to say to you, but I don't know |

A7sus4   𝄋 **Chorus**
                                      Cadd9   Em7

| how.   { Because } ‖ maybe |
| { I said } |

G   Em7   Cadd9   Em7   G   Em7

| you're gonna be the one that | saves me. | And after all |

Cadd9   Em7   G   Em7   Cadd9   Em7   *To Coda* ⊕

| | you're my won - der - wall. | |

1.

G   Em7   N.C.   A7sus4   **2.**   *D.S. al Coda*
                                                  G   Em7

                                                            | I said ‖

⊕ **Coda**

G   Em7   Cadd9   Em7   G   Em7

| I said | maybe | you're gonna be the one that ‖

                                   1., 2.   **3.**

Cadd9   Em7   G   Em7   G   Em7

‖: saves me. | You're gonna be the one that :‖ |

Outro   **1., 2., 3.**   **4.**

Cadd9   Em7   G   Em7   G   Em7

‖: | :‖ ‖

Yellow Submarine

Words and Music by John Lennon and Paul McCartney

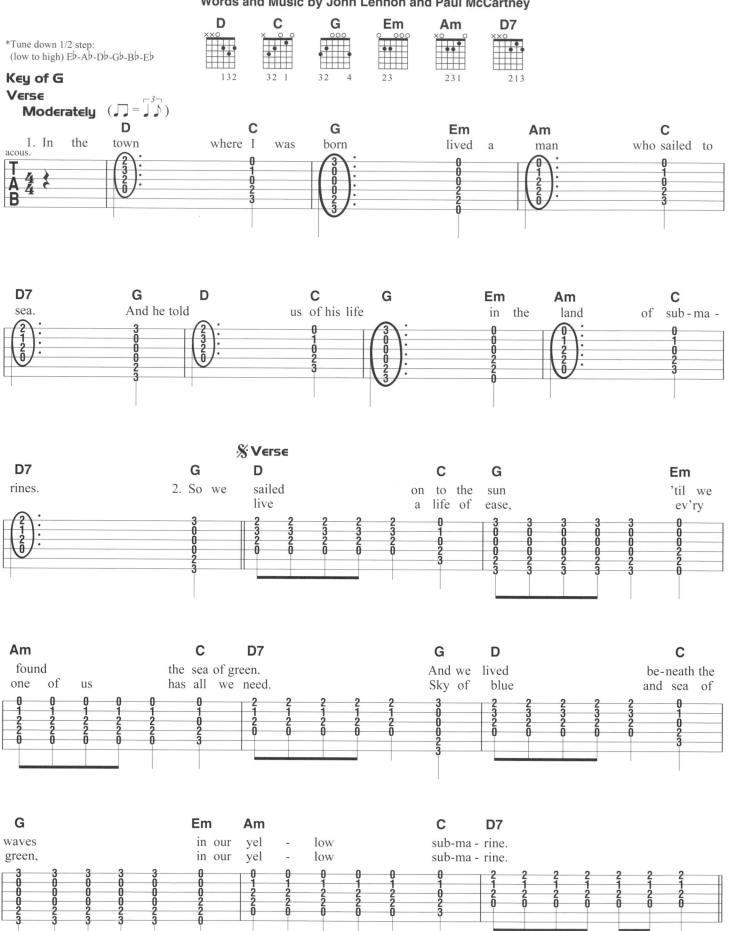

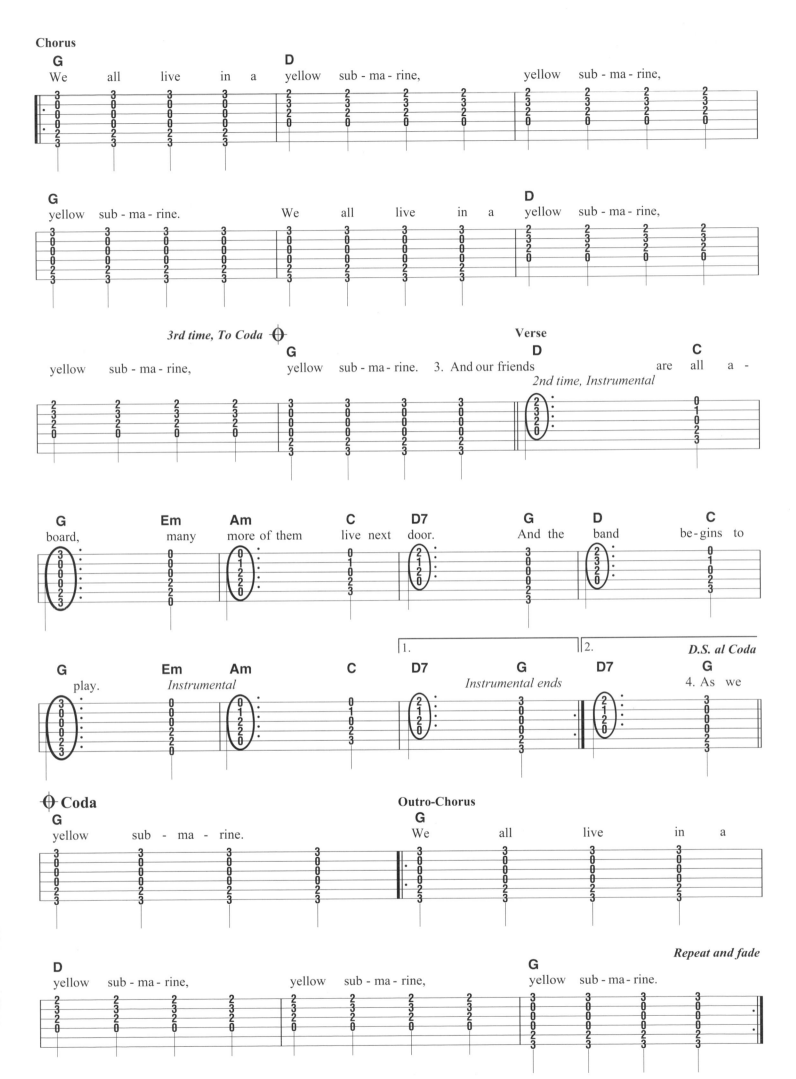

You Don't Mess Around with Jim

Words and Music by Jim Croce

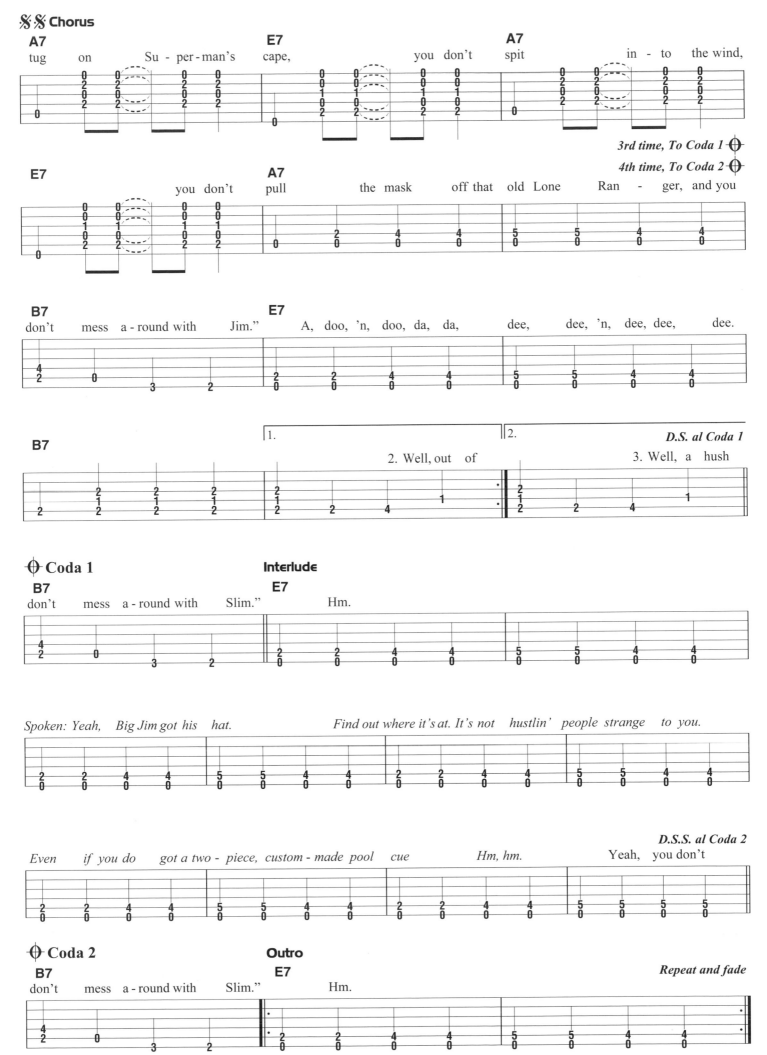

Rhythm Tab Legend

Rhythm Tab is a form of notation that adds rhythmic values to the traditional tab staff.

TABLATURE graphically represents the guitar fingerboard. Each horizontal line represents a string, and each number represents a fret. Rhythmic values are shown using ovals, stems, and dots.

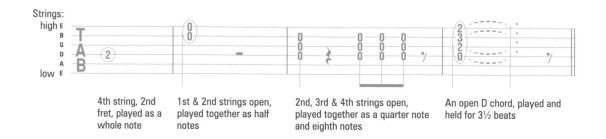

| 4th string, 2nd fret, played as a whole note | 1st & 2nd strings open, played together as half notes | 2nd, 3rd & 4th strings open, played together as a quarter note and eighth notes | An open D chord, played and held for 3½ beats |

Definitions for Special Guitar Notation

HALF-STEP BEND: Strike the note and bend up 1/2 step.

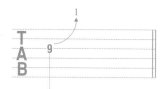

WHOLE-STEP BEND: Strike the note and bend up one step.

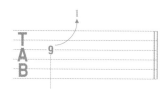

QUARTER-STEP BEND: Strike the note and bend up 1/4 step.

BEND AND RELEASE: Strike the note and bend up as indicated, then release back to the original note. Only the first note is struck.

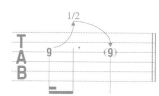

PRE-BEND: Bend the note as indicated, then strike it.

VIBRATO: The string is vibrated by rapidly bending and releasing the note with the fretting hand.

HAMMER-ON: Strike the first (lower) note with one finger, then sound the higher note (on the same string) with another finger by fretting it without picking.

PULL-OFF: Place both fingers on the notes to be sounded. Strike the first note, and without picking, pull the finger off to sound the second (lower) note.

LEGATO SLIDE: Strike the first note and then slide the same fret-hand finger up or down to the second note. The second note is not struck.

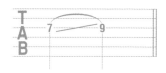

SHIFT SLIDE: Same as legato slide, except the second note is struck.

GRACE-NOTE SLUR: Strike the note and immediately hammer-on (pull-off or slide) as indicated.

TRILL: Very rapidly alternate between the notes indicated by continuously hammering on and pulling off.

NATURAL HARMONIC: Strike the note while the fret hand lightly touches the string directly over the fret indicated.

Harm.

MUFFLED STRINGS: A percussive sound is produced by laying the fret hand across the string(s) without depressing, and striking them with the pick hand.

PALM MUTING: The note is partially muted by the pick hand lightly touching the string(s) just before the bridge.

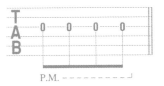

P.M. - - - - - - - -

Additional Musical Definitions

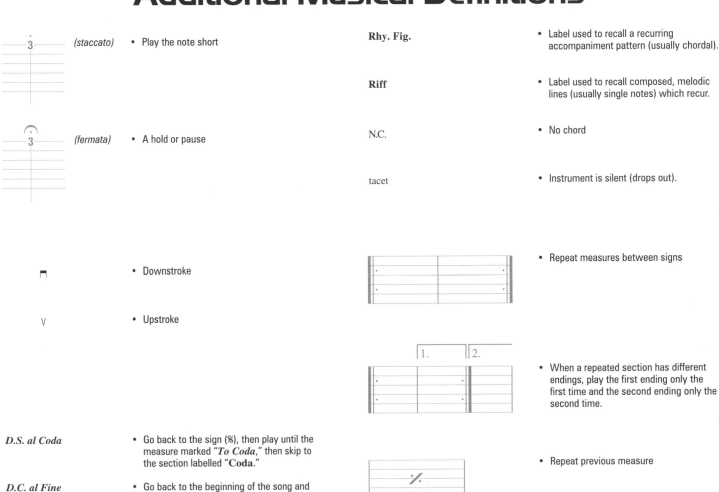

3 *(staccato)*	• Play the note short	
3 *(fermata)*	• A hold or pause	
⊓	• Downstroke	
V	• Upstroke	
D.S. al Coda	• Go back to the sign (𝄋), then play until the measure marked ***"To Coda,"*** then skip to the section labelled **"Coda."**	
D.C. al Fine	• Go back to the beginning of the song and play until the measure marked ***"Fine"*** (end).	

Rhy. Fig.	• Label used to recall a recurring accompaniment pattern (usually chordal).
Riff	• Label used to recall composed, melodic lines (usually single notes) which recur.
N.C.	• No chord
tacet	• Instrument is silent (drops out).
	• Repeat measures between signs
1. ‖ 2.	• When a repeated section has different endings, play the first ending only the first time and the second ending only the second time.
	• Repeat previous measure
	• Repeat previous two measures

NOTE: Tablature numbers in parentheses are used when:
• The note is sustained, but a new articulation begins (such as a hammer-on, pull-off, slide, or bend), or
• A bend is released.

REALLY EASY GUITAR

Easy-to-follow charts to get you playing right away are presented in these collections of arrangements in chords, lyrics and basic tab for all guitarists.

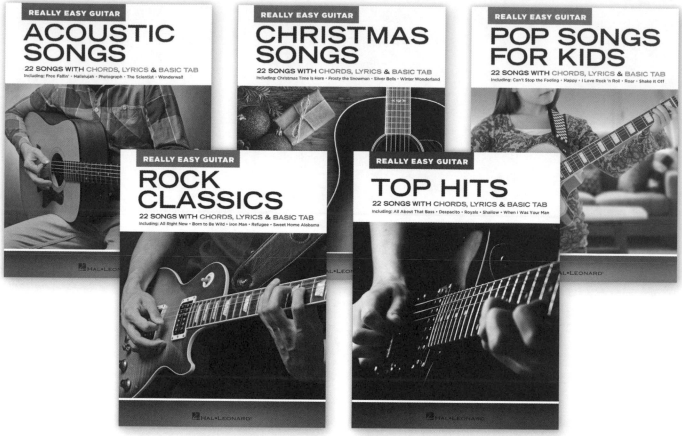

ACOUSTIC CLASSICS
22 songs: Angie • Best of My Love • Dust in the Wind • Fire and Rain • A Horse with No Name • Layla • More Than a Feeling • Night Moves • Patience • Time in a Bottle • Wanted Dead or Alive • and more.
00300600 .... $9.99

ACOUSTIC SONGS
22 songs: Free Fallin' • Good Riddance (Time of Your Life) • Hallelujah • I'm Yours • Losing My Religion • Mr. Jones • Photograph • Riptide • The Scientist • Wonderwall • and more.
00286663 .... $10.99

ADELE
22 songs: All I Ask • Chasing Pavements • Daydreamer • Easy On Me • Hello • I Drink Wine • Love in the Dark • Lovesong • Make You Feel My Love • Turning Tables • Water Under the Bridge • and more.
00399557 .... $12.99

THE BEATLES FOR KIDS
14 songs: All You Need Is Love • Blackbird • Good Day Sunshine • Here Comes the Sun • I Want to Hold Your Hand • Let It Be • With a Little Help from My Friends • Yellow Submarine • and more.
00346031 .... $10.99

CHRISTMAS CLASSICS
22 Christmas carols: Away in a Manger • Deck the Hall • It Came upon the Midnight Clear • Jingle Bells • Silent Night • The Twelve Days of Christmas • We Wish You a Merry Christmas • and more.
00348327 .... $9.99

CHRISTMAS SONGS
22 holiday favorites: Blue Christmas • Christmas Time Is Here • Frosty the Snowman • Have Yourself a Merry Little Christmas • Mary, Did You Know? • Silver Bells • Winter Wonderland • and more.
00294775 .... $9.99

THE DOORS
22 songs: Break on Through to the Other Side • Hello, I Love You (Won't You Tell Me Your Name?) • L.A. Woman • Light My Fire • Love Her Madly • People Are Strange • Riders on the Storm • Touch Me • and more.
00345890 .... $9.99

BILLIE EILISH
14 songs: All the Good Girls Go to Hell • Bad Guy • Everything I Wanted • Idontwannabeyouanymore • No Time to Die • Ocean Eyes • Six Feet Under • Wish You Were Gay • and more.
00346351 .... $10.99

POP SONGS FOR KIDS
22 songs: Brave • Can't Stop the Feeling • Happy • I Love Rock 'N Roll • Let It Go • Roar • Shake It Off • We Got the Beat • and more.
00286698 .... $10.99

ROCK CLASSICS
22 songs: All Right Now • Born to Be Wild • Don't Fear the Reaper • Hey Joe • Iron Man • Old Time Rock & Roll • Refugee • Sweet Home Alabama • You Shook Me All Night Long • and more.
00286699 .... $10.99

TAYLOR SWIFT
22 hits: Back to December • Cardigan • Exile • Look What You Made Me Do • Mean • The One • Our Song • Safe & Sound • Teardrops on My Guitar • We Are Never Ever Getting Back Together • White Horse • You Need to Calm Down • and more.
00356881 .... $10.99

TOP HITS
22 hits: All About That Bass • All of Me • Despacito • Love Yourself • Royals • Say Something • Shallow • Someone like You • This Is Me • A Thousand Years • When I Was Your Man • and more.
00300599 .... $9.99

halleonard.com

THE BOOK SERIES
FOR EASY GUITAR

THE ACOUSTIC BOOK
00702251 Easy Guitar $16.99

THE BEATLES BOOK
00699266 Easy Guitar $19.95

THE BLUES BOOK – 2ND ED.
00702104 Easy Guitar $16.95

THE CHRISTMAS CAROLS BOOK
00702186 Easy Guitar $14.95

THE CHRISTMAS CLASSICS BOOK
00702200 Easy Guitar $14.95

THE ERIC CLAPTON BOOK
00702056 Easy Guitar $18.95

THE CLASSIC COUNTRY BOOK
00702018 Easy Guitar $19.99

THE CLASSIC ROCK BOOK
00698977 Easy Guitar $19.95

THE CONTEMPORARY CHRISTIAN BOOK
00702195 Easy Guitar $17.99

THE COUNTRY CLASSIC FAVORITES BOOK
00702238 Easy Guitar $19.99

HAL•LEONARD®
www.halleonard.com

Prices, contents, and availability
subject to change without notice.

Disney characters and artwork © Disney Enterprises, Inc.

THE DISNEY SONGS BOOK
00702168 Easy Guitar $19.95

THE FOLKSONGS BOOK
00702180 Easy Guitar $15.99

THE GOSPEL SONGS BOOK
00702157 Easy Guitar $16.99

THE HYMN BOOK
00702142 Easy Guitar $14.99

THE ELVIS BOOK
00702163 Easy Guitar $19.95

THE ROCK CLASSICS BOOK
00702055 Easy Guitar $19.99

THE WORSHIP BOOK
00702247 Easy Guitar $15.99

easy GUITAR play along

Audio Access Included

INCLUDES TAB

The *Easy Guitar Play Along*® series features streamlined transcriptions of your favorite songs. Just follow the tab, listen to the audio to hear how the guitar should sound, and then play along using the backing tracks. Playback tools are provided for slowing down the tempo without changing pitch and looping challenging parts. The melody and lyrics are included in the book so that you can sing or simply follow along.

1. ROCK CLASSICS
Jailbreak • Living After Midnight • Mississippi Queen • Rocks Off • Runnin' Down a Dream • Smoke on the Water • Strutter • Up Around the Bend.
00702560 Book/CD Pack....... $14.99

2. ACOUSTIC TOP HITS
About a Girl • I'm Yours • The Lazy Song • The Scientist • 21 Guns • Upside Down • What I Got • Wonderwall.
00702569 Book/CD Pack....... $14.99

3. ROCK HITS
All the Small Things • Best of You • Brain Stew (The Godzilla Remix) • Californication • Island in the Sun • Plush • Smells Like Teen Spirit • Use Somebody.
00702570 Book/CD Pack....... $14.99

4. ROCK 'N' ROLL
Blue Suede Shoes • I Get Around • I'm a Believer • Jailhouse Rock • Oh, Pretty Woman • Peggy Sue • Runaway • Wake Up Little Susie.
00702572 Book/CD Pack....... $14.99

6. CHRISTMAS SONGS
Have Yourself a Merry Little Christmas • A Holly Jolly Christmas • The Little Drummer Boy • Run Rudolph Run • Santa Claus Is Comin' to Town • Silver and Gold • Sleigh Ride • Winter Wonderland.
00101879 Book/CD Pack......... $14.99

7. BLUES SONGS FOR BEGINNERS
Come On (Part 1) • Double Trouble • Gangster of Love • I'm Ready • Let Me Love You Baby • Mary Had a Little Lamb • San-Ho-Zay • T-Bone Shuffle.
00103235 Book/
        Online Audio.......... $17.99

9. ROCK SONGS FOR BEGINNERS
Are You Gonna Be My Girl • Buddy Holly • Everybody Hurts • In Bloom • Otherside • The Rock Show • Santa Monica • When I Come Around.
00103255 Book/CD Pack..... $14.99

10. GREEN DAY
Basket Case • Boulevard of Broken Dreams • Good Riddance (Time of Your Life) • Holiday • Longview • 21 Guns • Wake Me up When September Ends • When I Come Around.
00122322 Book/
        Online Audio........ $16.99

11. NIRVANA
All Apologies • Come As You Are • Heart Shaped Box • Lake of Fire • Lithium • The Man Who Sold the World • Rape Me • Smells Like Teen Spirit.
00122325 Book/
        Online Audio........ $17.99

13. AC/DC
Back in Black • Dirty Deeds Done Dirt Cheap • For Those About to Rock (We Salute You) • Hells Bells • Highway to Hell • Rock and Roll Ain't Noise Pollution • T.N.T. • You Shook Me All Night Long.
14042895 Book/
        Online Audio........ $17.99

14. JIMI HENDRIX – SMASH HITS
All Along the Watchtower • Can You See Me • Crosstown Traffic • Fire • Foxey Lady • Hey Joe • Manic Depression • Purple Haze • Red House • Remember • Stone Free • The Wind Cries Mary.
00130591 Book/
        Online Audio........ $24.99

HAL•LEONARD®

www.halleonard.com

Prices, contents, and availability subject to change without notice.